1ST GRADE PHONICS
Unit 4
Phonograms 50–72

MW01593374

TABLE OF CONTENTS

IMPORTANT: Please refer to the Teacher Guide for specific scripts, procedures, and words that are represented by pictures.

Throughout this Unit, learners will scan QR codes. Be careful they scan each code individually.

LEARN

- VCV syllable division
- Trigraphs
- Final stable syllables

VOCABULARY

trigraph
prefix
final stable syllables

DAILY PAGE GOALS

Day	Complete	Day	Complete	Day	Complete
1	ii–8	7	36–43	13	69–75
2	9–18	8	44–50	14	76–83
3	19–27	9	51–60	15	84–90
4	28–31	10	61–64	16	91–94
5	32–33	11	65–66	17	95–96
6	34–35	12	67–68	18	97–98

1. WHAT DO ph, oe, AND oa SAY?

Learn:

- Write and say the sounds for multi-letter phonograms **ph**, **oe**, and **oa**.

- Divide and read two-syllable words.

Listen and review.
Mark ☒ when done.

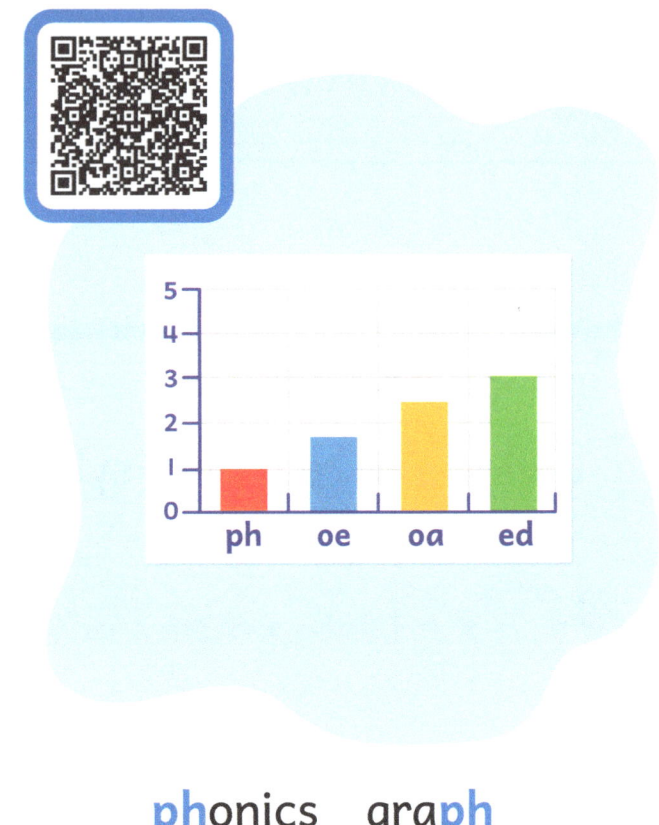

phonics   graph

Write and say the sound.
Underline the multi-letter phonograms.

ph
ph

2

ob**oe**   her**oe**s

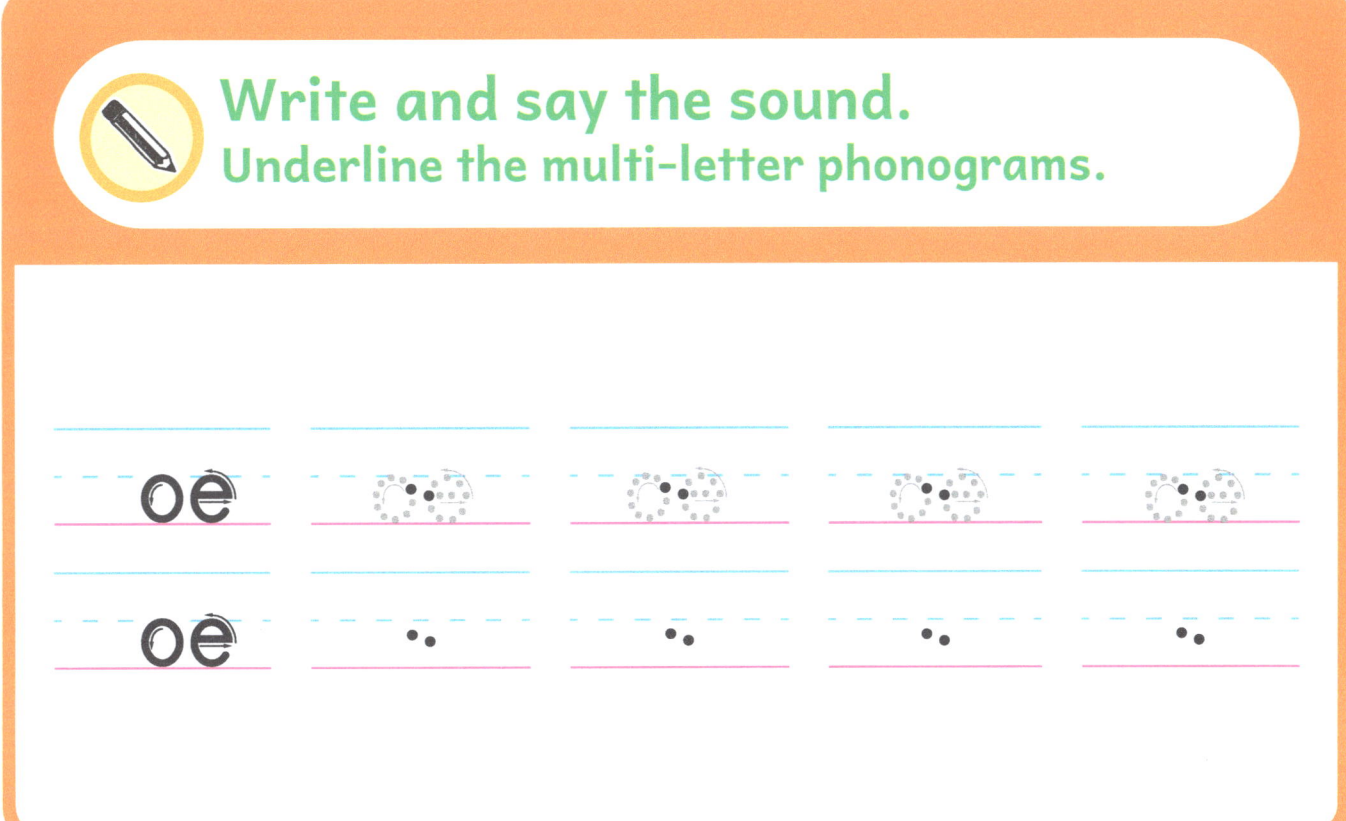

✏️ Write and say the sound.
Underline the multi-letter phonograms.

oe

oe

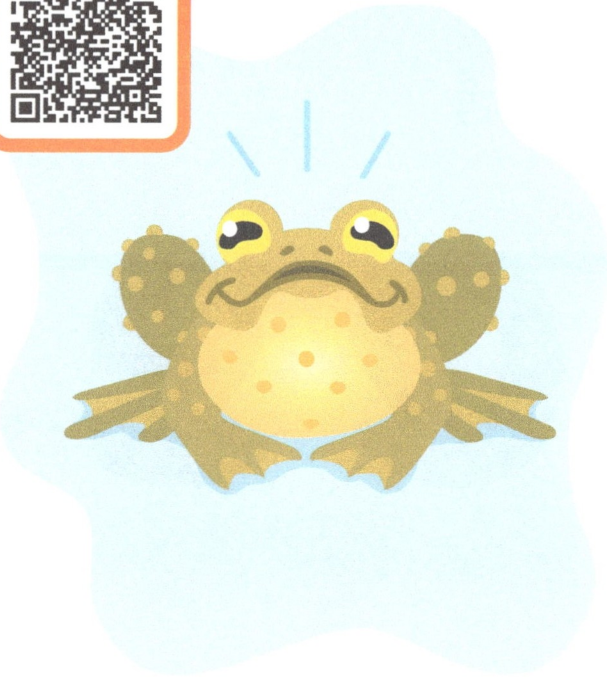

t**oa**d   cr**oa**k

✏️ Write and say the sound.
Underline the multi-letter phonograms.

oa

oa

 # Read and write the words.

phone

1)

graph

2)

photo

3)

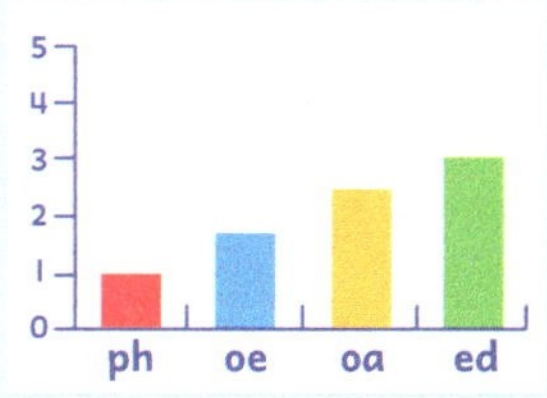

ph   oe   oa   ed

toe

4)

Joe

5)

toes

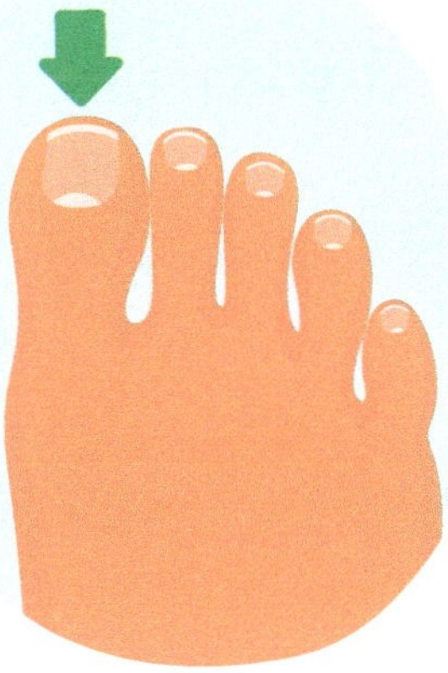

6)

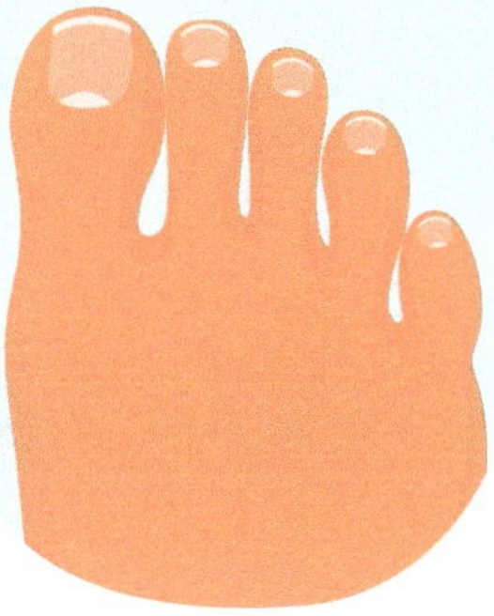

| boat | soap | coach |

7)

8)

9)

WORKING WITH WORDS

You have been reading two-syllable words with open and closed syllables. Now, you will read two-syllable words with more syllable types. We will add a new step.

1 – Underline any multi-letter phonograms. The letters cannot be split apart.

r <u>oo</u> s t <u>er</u>   s e <u>qu</u> i n

2 – Mark the vowels, mark the consonants, and divide.

```
  v c | c v          v | c v
r oo s | t er       s e | qu i n
```

3 – Identify vowel team syllables and r-controlled syllables.

v c	c v	v	c v
r <u>oo</u> s	t <u>er</u>	s e	<u>qu</u> i n
Vowel team	R-Controlled	Open	Closed

Mark, divide, and read the VCV and VCCV words.

Remember, underline the multi-letter phonograms first.

fiber	zipper	panther
gopher	mentor	acorn
bamboo	igloo	essay
daisy	canteen	enjoy

Listen to and write the phonograms.
Underline any multi-letter phonograms.

SCORE   CORRECT   RESCORE

2. WHAT DO *ea*, *ed*, AND **wor** SAY?

Learn:

- Write and say the sounds for multi-letter phonograms **ea**, **ed**, and **wor**.

- Divide and read two-syllable words.

Listen and review.
Mark ⊠ when done.

WORKING WITH SOUNDS

READING PHONOGRAM REVIEW

je**ea**ns sw**ea**ter w**ea**r

Vowel team **ea** makes its first sound most of the time.

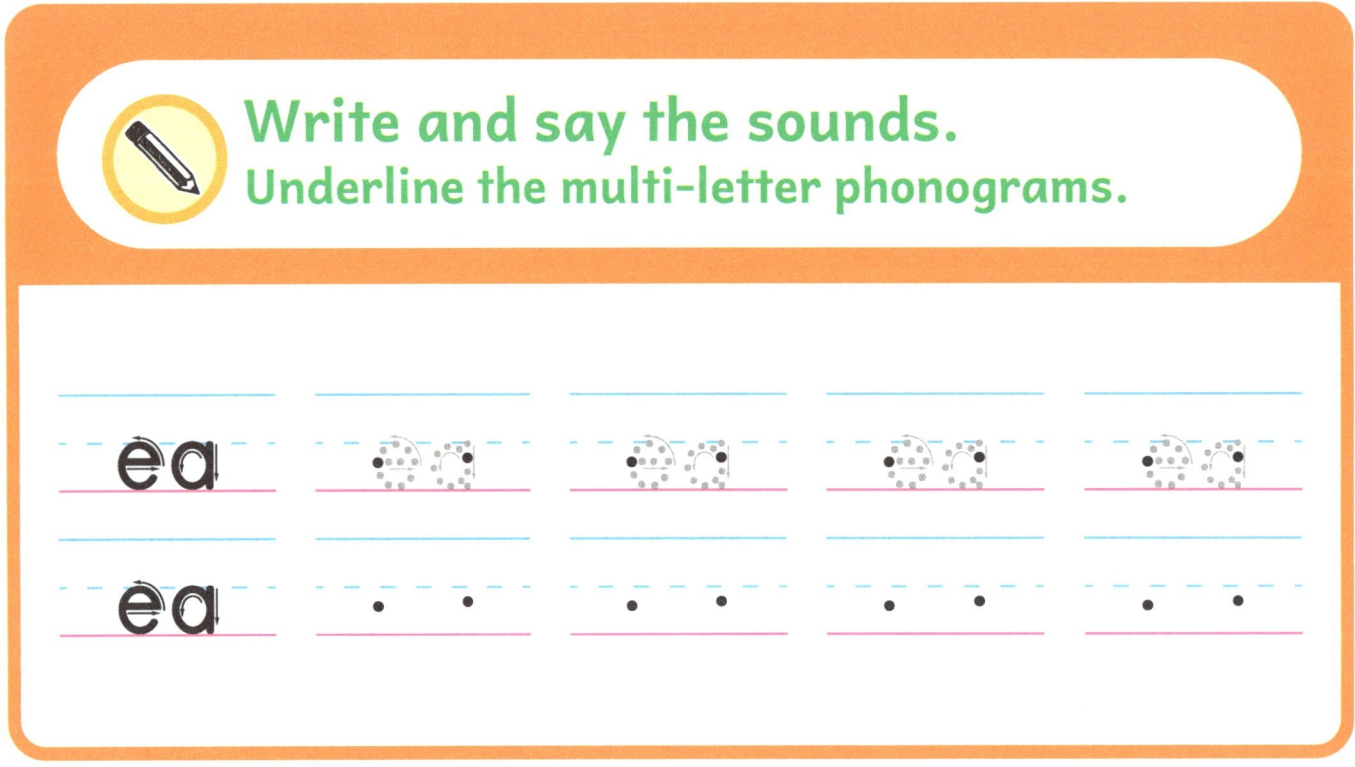

Write and say the sounds.
Underline the multi-letter phonograms.

ea

ea

10

dust**ed** clean**ed** work**ed**

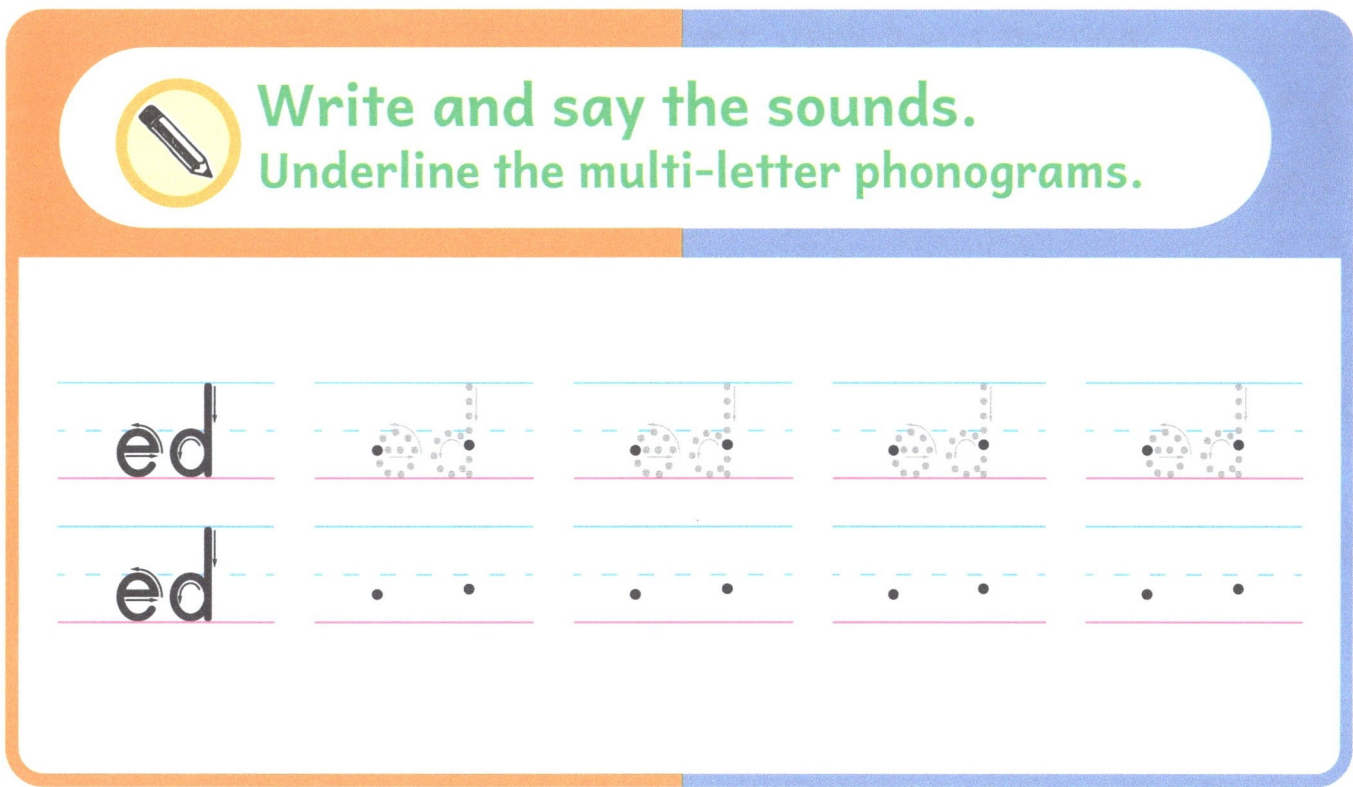

Write and say the sounds.
Underline the multi-letter phonograms.

ed

ed

wor

worthy   artw**or**k

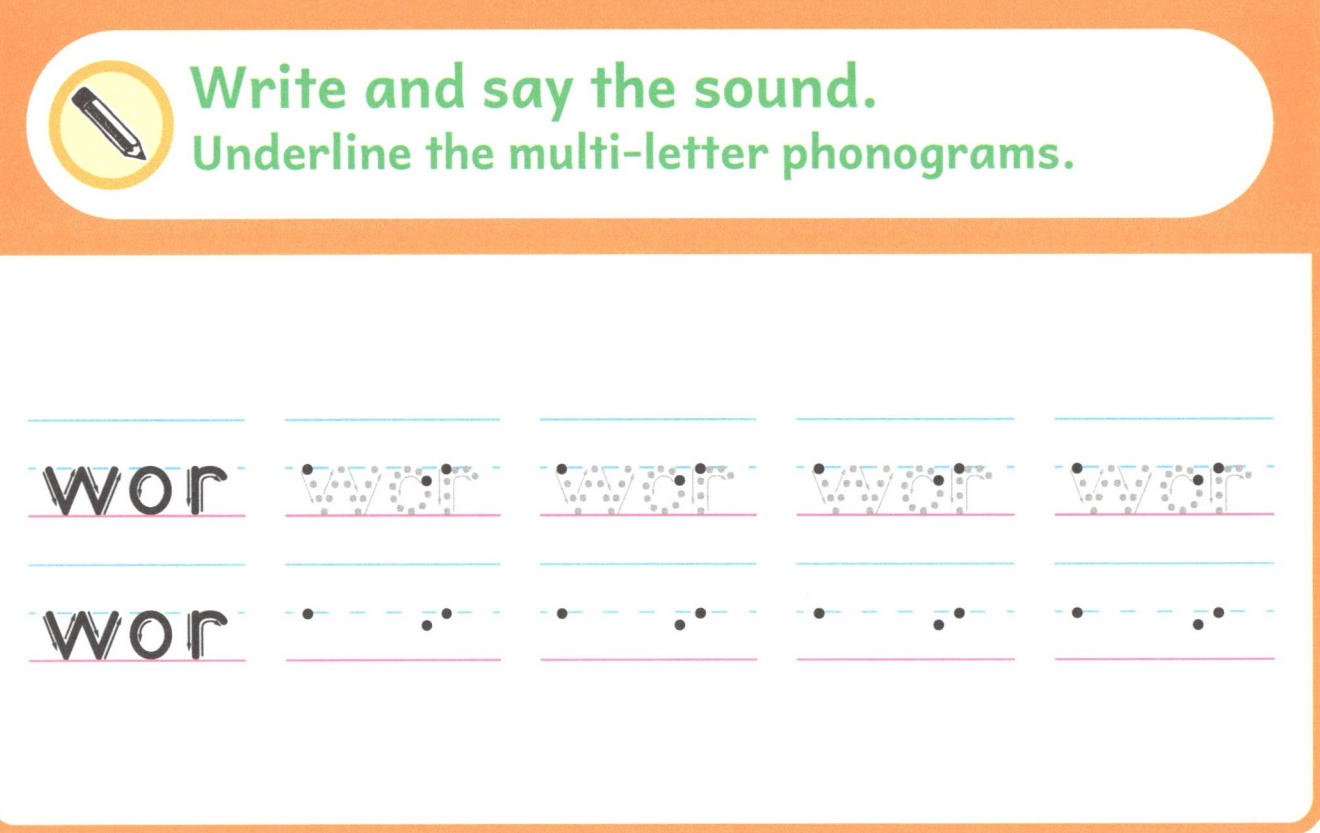

Write and say the sound.
Underline the multi-letter phonograms.

wor wor wor wor wor

wor

12

Read and write the words.
First sound of **ea**

leaf   clean   eat

1)

2)

3)

Read and write the words.
Second sound of **ea**

head   thread   spread

4)

5)

6)

✏️ Read and write the words.
Third sound of **ea**

break	bear	great

7)

- - - - - - -
_____

8)

- - - - - - -
_____

9)

- - - - - - -
_____

✏️ Read and write the words.

jumped	rained	pulled

10)

- - - - - - -
_____

11)

- - - - - - -
_____

12)

- - - - - - -
_____

worm   work   world

13)

14)

15)

WORKING WITH WORDS

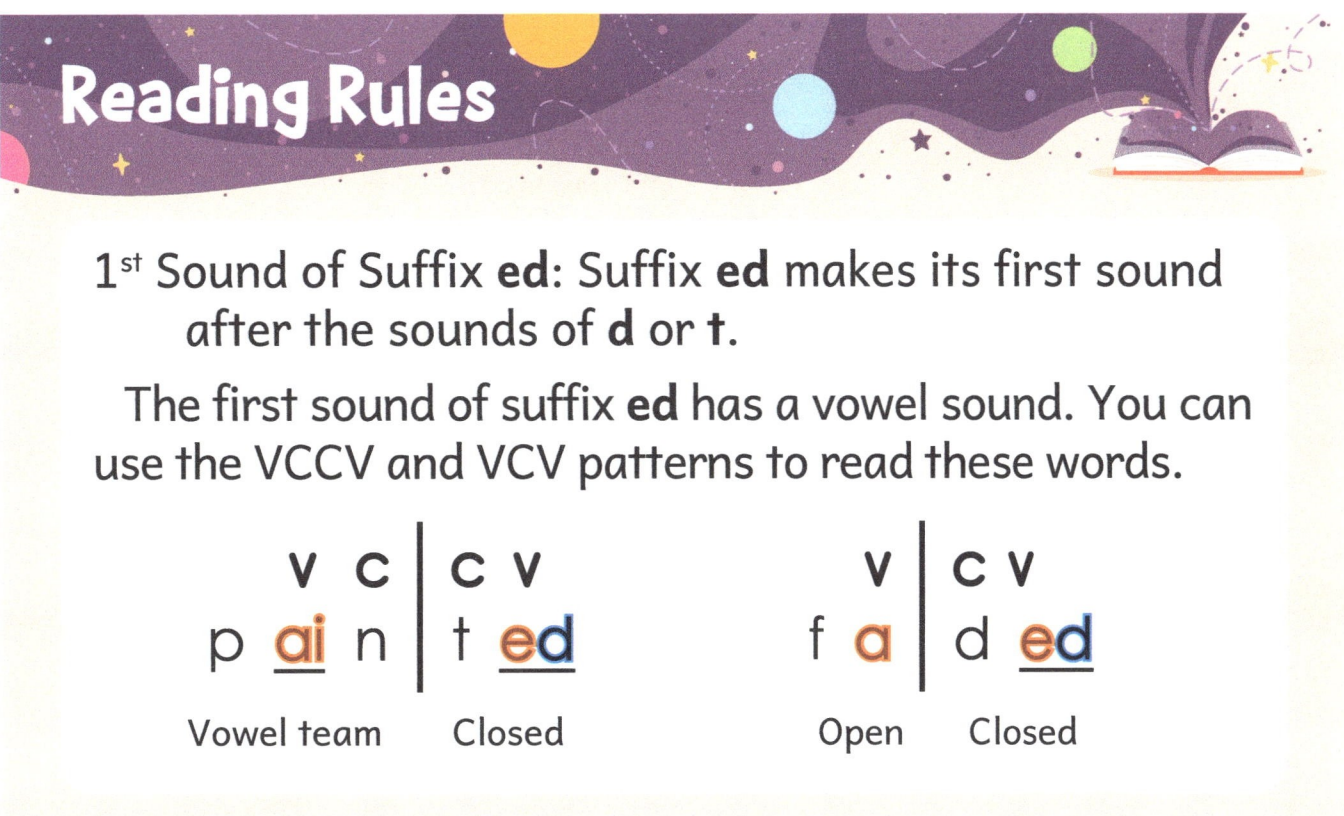

Reading Rules

1st Sound of Suffix **ed**: Suffix **ed** makes its first sound after the sounds of **d** or **t**.

The first sound of suffix **ed** has a vowel sound. You can use the VCCV and VCV patterns to read these words.

v c	c v
p ai n	t ed
Vowel team	Closed

v	c v
f a	d ed
Open	Closed

Mark, divide, and read the VCV and VCCV words.

Remember, underline the multi-letter phonograms first.

muted

sided

ended

tested

hinted

rated

floated

added

needed

landed

waited

melted

Listen to and write the phonograms.
Underline any multi-letter phonograms.

SCORE   CORRECT   RESCORE

ACTIVITY: Everyday Words

Read, trace, and write the words.

Read	Trace	Write
head	head	
read	read	
work	work	
asked	asked	
called	called	
played	played	
showed	showed	
helped	helped	
wanted	wanted	
handed	handed	

Learn:

- Write and say the sounds for multi-letter phonograms **ear**, **igh**, and **ie**.

- Divide and read two-syllable words.

Vocabulary:

trigraph [′trī grăf] – three letters that make one sound

Listen and review.
Mark ☒ when done.

The next phonogram is a trigraph. A **trigraph** has three letters that make one sound.

earth   res**ear**ch

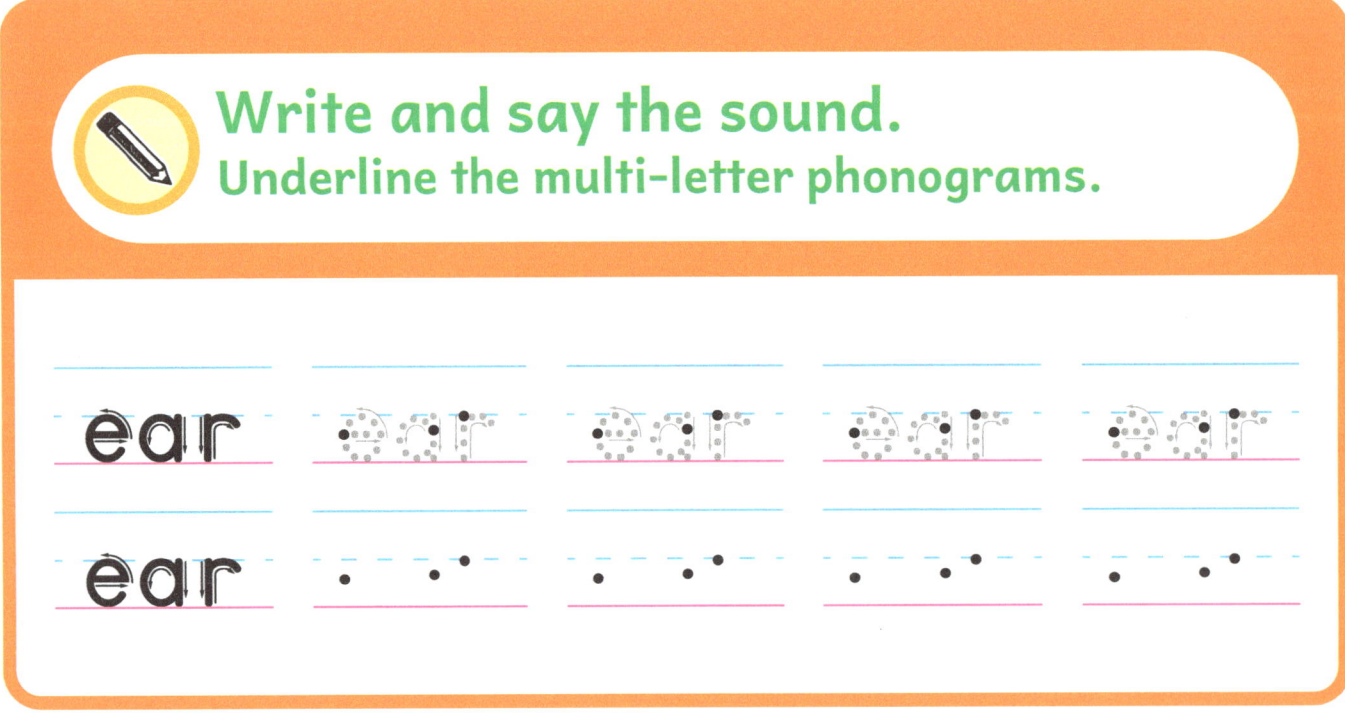

Write and say the sound.
Underline the multi-letter phonograms.

ear   ear   ear   ear   ear

ear

igh

m**igh**ty   h**igh**

Write and say the sound.
Underline the multi-letter phonograms.

igh
igh

p**ie**   shi**e**ld

✏️ Write and say the sounds.
Underline the multi-letter phonograms.

ie   ie   ie   ie   ie

ie

 ## Read and write the words.

learn

pearl

search

1)

2)

3)

night

right

bright

4)

5)

6)

Reading Rules

One-Syllable words with **ie**: Vowel team **ie** usually makes its first sound at the end of a one-syllable base word and in the suffixes **ies** and **ied**.

t**ie**   pr**ie**d

Vowel team **ie** makes its second sound in the middle of a one-syllable base word.

shr**ie**k

Read and write the words.
First sound of **ie**

tie   cried   fries

7)   **8)**   **9)**

Read and write the words.
Second sound of **ie**

shield   field   yield

10)   **11)**   **12)**

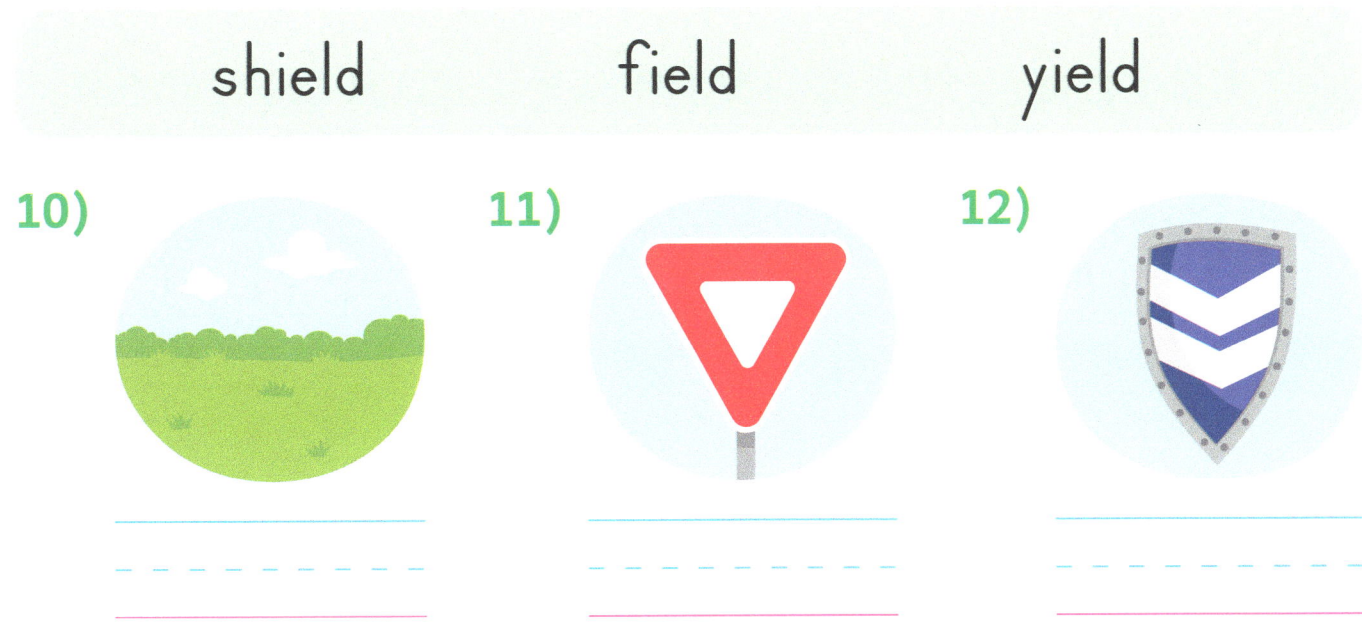

Multi-Syllable words with **ie**: Vowel team **ie** usually makes its second sound in a multi-syllable word.

v c	c v
b u n	n **ie** s
Closed	Vowel Team

v	c v
c **oo**	k **ie**
Vowel Team	Vowel Team

 **Mark, divide, and read the VCV and VCCV words.**

Remember, underline the multi-letter phonograms first.

tidied   envied   puppies

ladies   relief

brownie   Maggie   Archie

 **Listen to and write the phonograms.**
Underline any multi-letter phonograms.

SCORE   CORRECT   RESCORE

PHONOGRAM REVIEW

1)  g nk ng

2)  oo oa o

3)  igh ie ee

4)  ea ee ay

5)  ed d ew

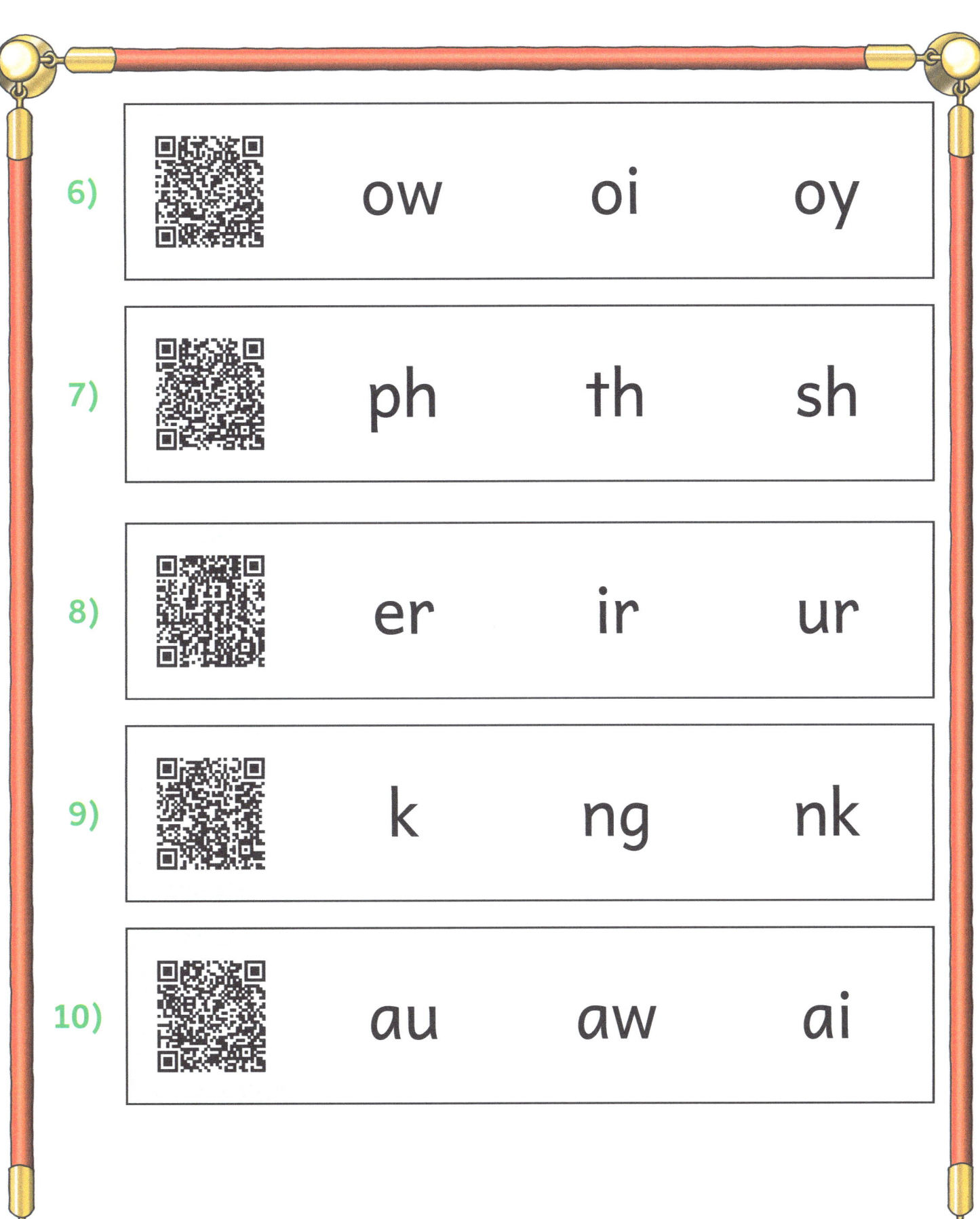

6) ow   oi   oy

7) ph   th   sh

8) er   ir   ur

9) k   ng   nk

10) au   aw   ai

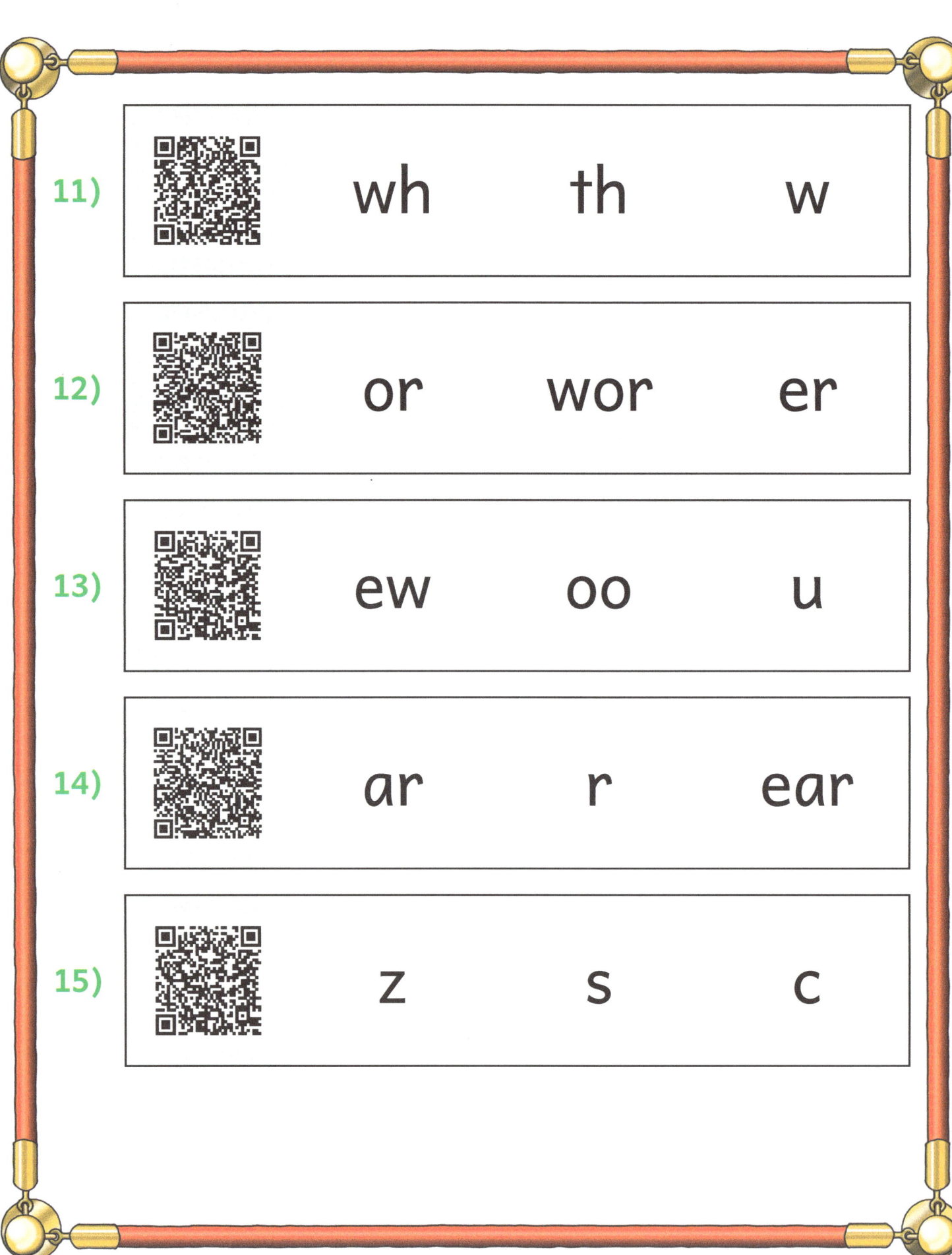

11) wh   th   w

12) or   wor   er

13) ew   oo   u

14) ar   r   ear

15) z   s   c

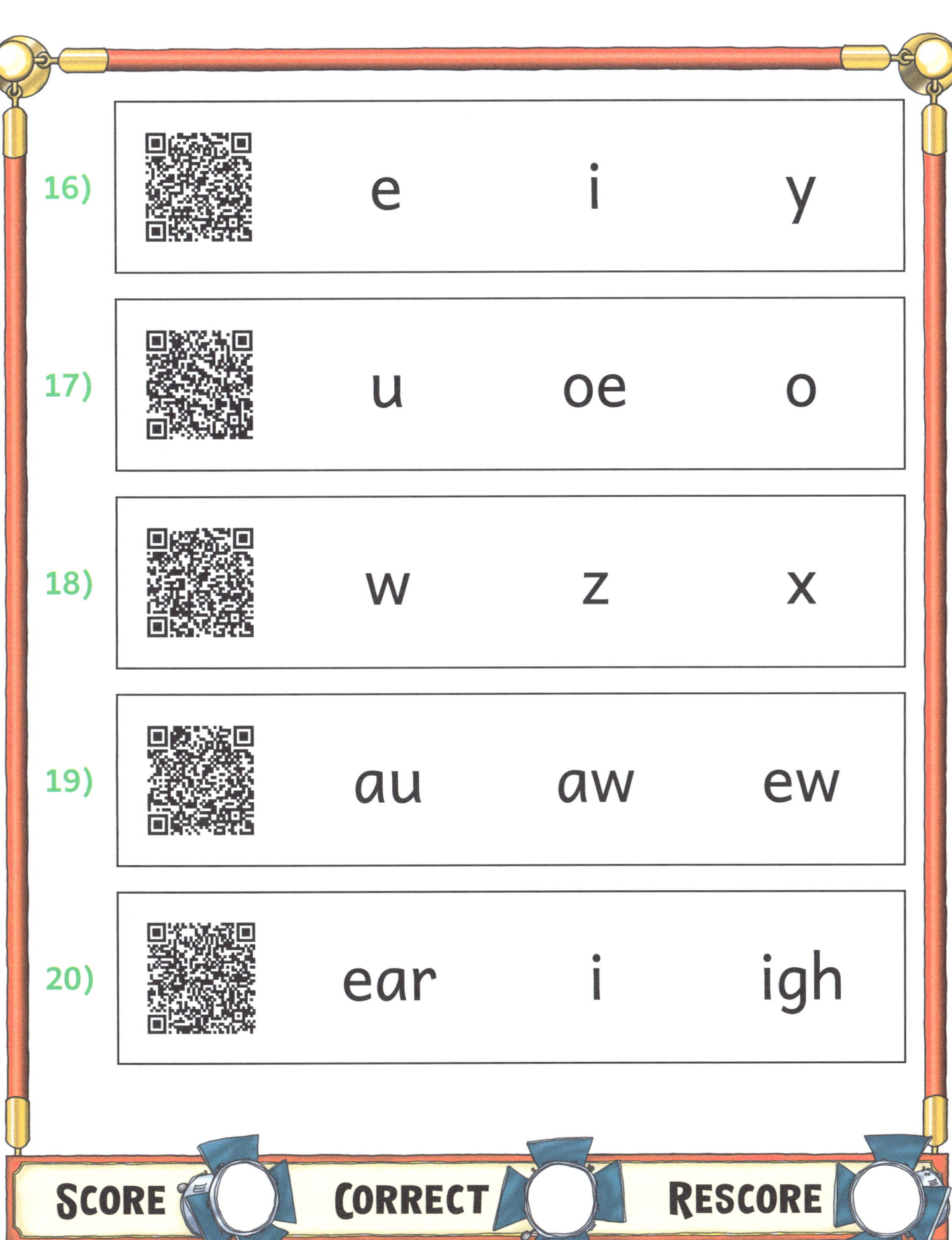

16) e   i   y

17) u   oe   o

18) w   z   x

19) au   aw   ew

20) ear   i   igh

SCORE   CORRECT   RESCORE

READER 5: "A Day at the Pier"

Before you read, practice these words.

 **Read and trace the words.**

1) pier

2) shriek

3) heard

4) treat

5) head

6) bread

7) trophy

8) photo

9) world

Reader 5

A Day at the Pier

Choose the correct answers.

10) What kind of animal is Ottie?
- ○ dog
- ○ otter
- ○ toad

11) What trick did Bix do?
- ○ baked pies
- ○ leaped on the pier
- ○ stacked things

12) What did Joe do with his pie?
- ○ shared it with Erm
- ○ saved it for later
- ○ ate it all in one bite

Phonogram Test 10

Listen to and write the correct phonograms.
Underline any multi-letter phonograms.

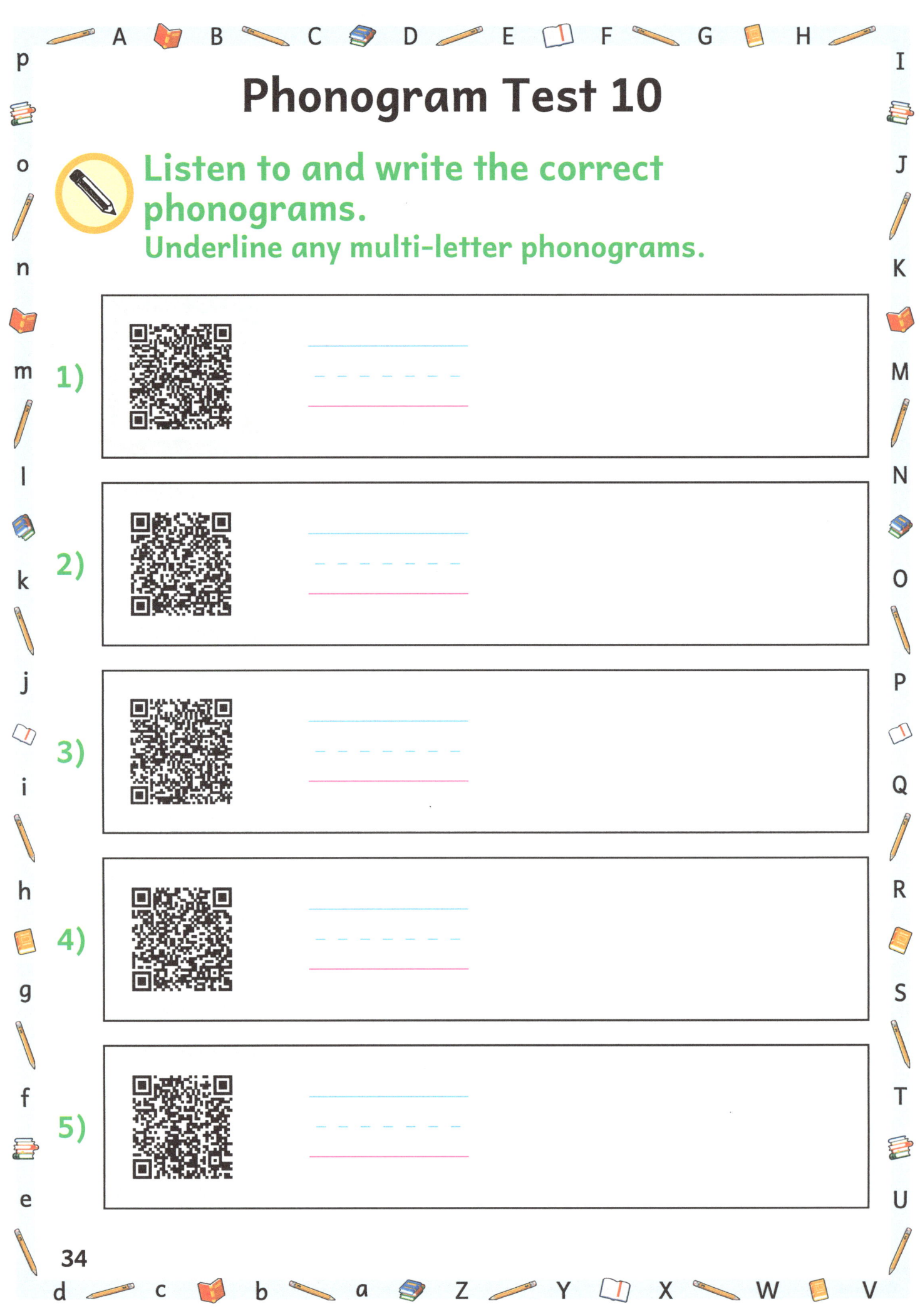

1)

2)

3)

4)

5)

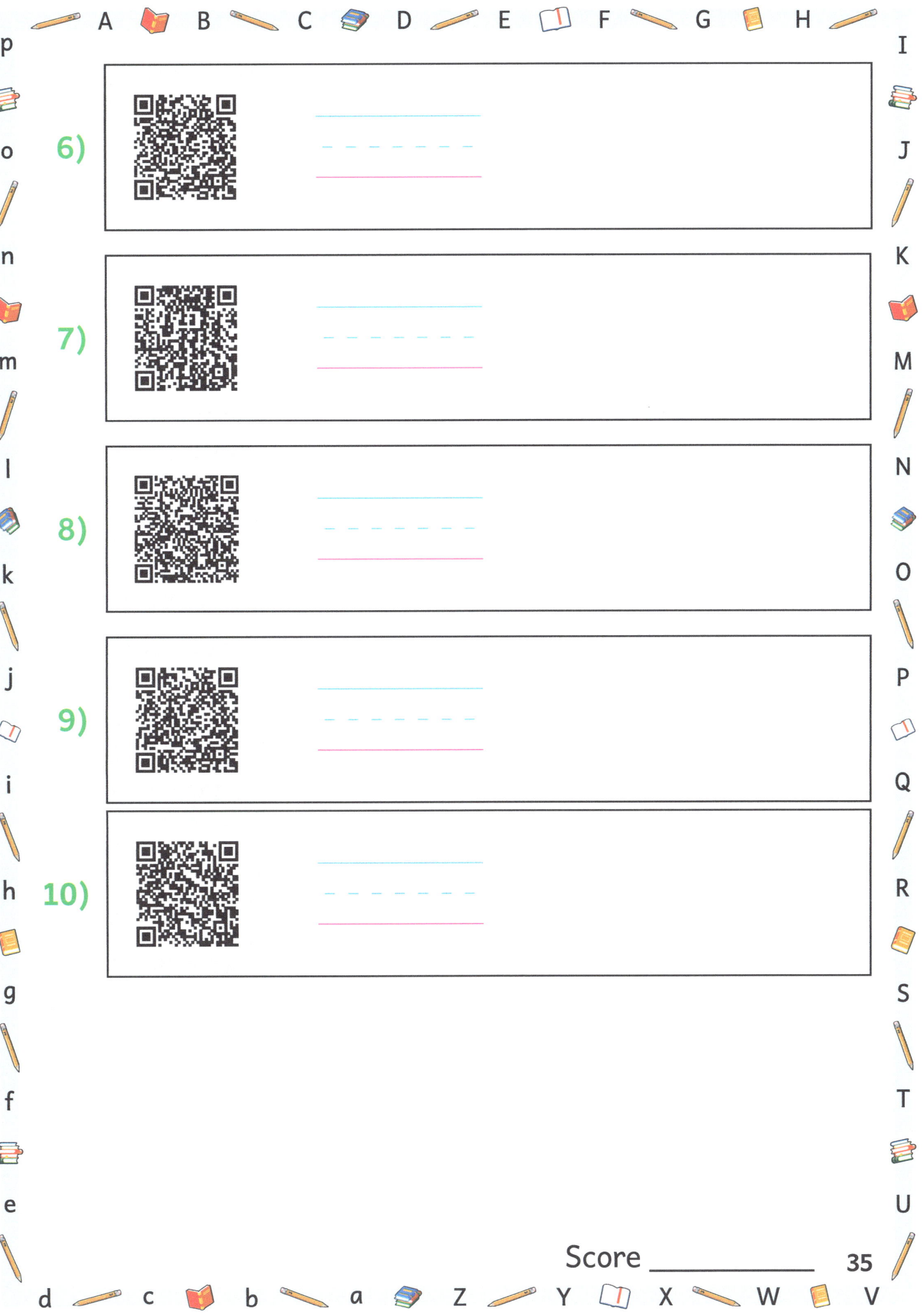

4. WHAT DO **wr** AND **ey** SAY?

Learn:

- Write and say the sounds for multi-letter phonograms **wr** and **ey**.

- Read two-syllable words.

**Listen and review.
Mark ☒ when done.**

wrist　**wr**ap

Write and say the sound.
Underline the multi-letter phonograms.

wr　wr　wr　wr　wr

wr

monk**ey**   ob**ey**

Write and say the sounds.
Underline the multi-letter phonograms.

ey   ey   ey   ey   ey

ey

 # Read and write the words.

write   wrench   wrong

1)

- - - - - - -
----

2)

- - - - - - -
----

3)

- - - - - - -

 # Circle the correct answers.

4) Which TWO words use **ey**?

Vowel team **ey** makes its first sound most of the time.

✏️ **Read and write the words.**
First sound of ey

| key | chimney | jersey |

5)

6)

7)

✏️ **Read and write the words.**
Second sound of ey

| hey | they | survey |

8)

9)

10)

WORKING WITH WORDS

Some words break the rules for syllable types. The consonants next to the vowels are more important.

Reading Rules

O before **m**, **n**, or **v**: The letter **o** often makes the short **u** sound before the sounds of **m**, **n**, or **v**.

from   son

These kinds of words may not follow the rules for syllable divisions. You can draw an arrow to help you remember how the consonant changes the vowel.

v c | c v
b l o s | s o m
Closed

v | c v
m o | n ey
Vowel Team

11) honey

12) almond

13) shovel

42

WRITING PHONOGRAM REVIEW

✏️ **Listen to and write the phonograms.**
Underline any multi-letter phonograms.

Learn:

- Write and say the sounds for multi-letter phonograms **dge** and **tch**.

- Read two-syllable words.

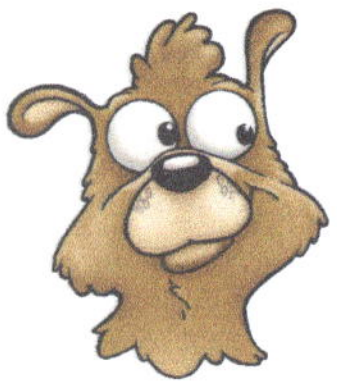

Listen and review.
Mark ☒ when done.

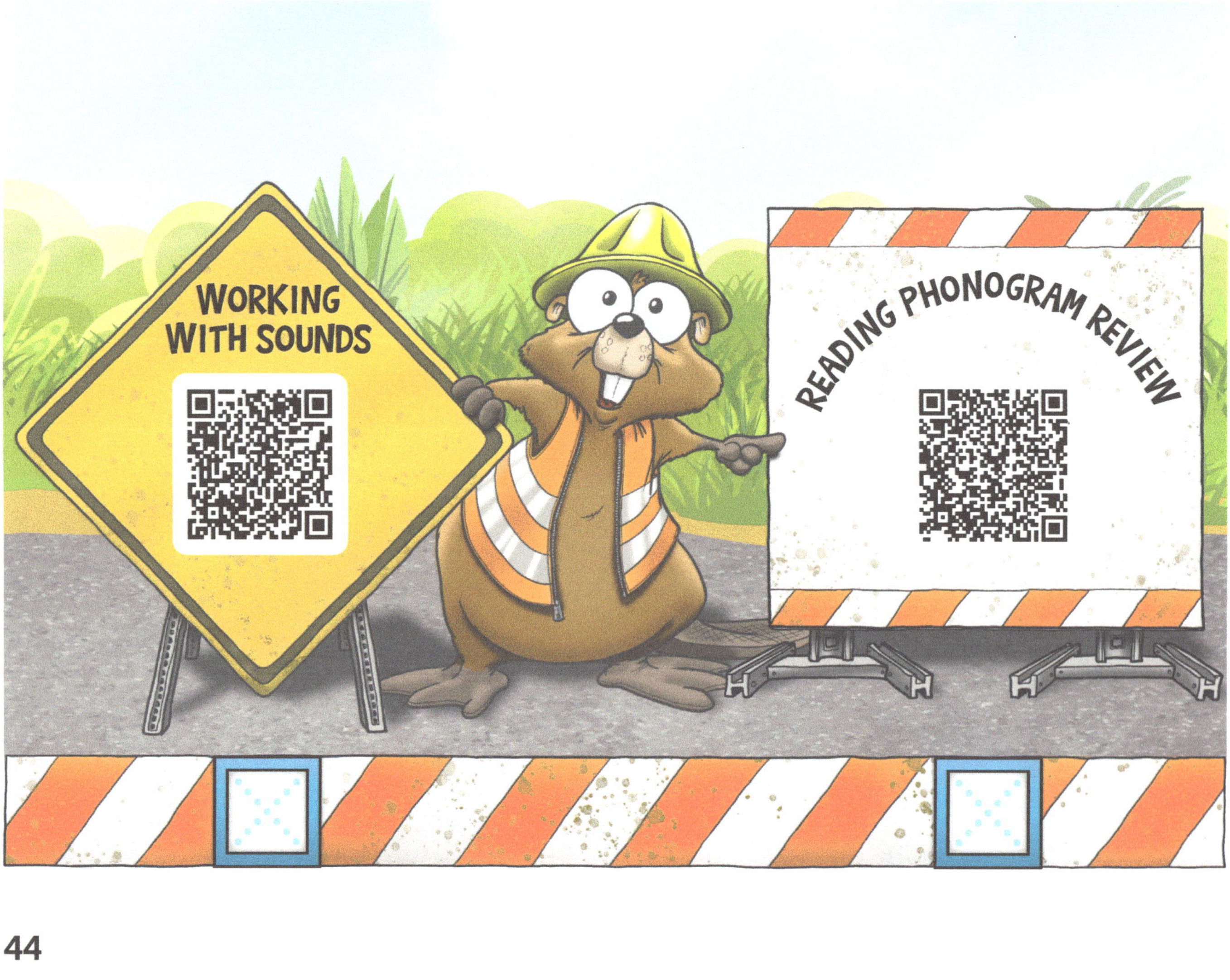

WORKING WITH SOUNDS

READING PHONOGRAM REVIEW

dge

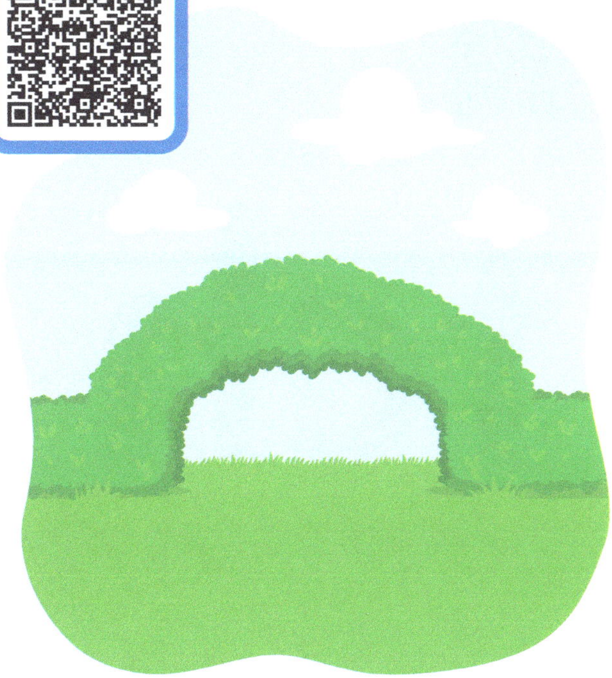

he**dge**   bri**dge**

dge

dge

tch

pi**tch**   ca**tch**

Write and say the sound.
Underline the multi-letter phonograms.

tch   tch   tch   tch   tch

tch

 # Read and write the words.

judge   badge   fridge

1)   2)   3)

_____

_____

_____

watch   hatch   scratch

4)   5)   6)

_____

_____

_____

WORKING WITH WORDS

We will keep looking at words that do not follow the rules for syllable types.

Phonograms **ck** and **tch** are used after a short vowel. Use them as clues. They will help you remember the vowel is short.

j a **ck** e t   r a **tch** e t

Circle the correct answers.
Which pictures show the words?

7) kitchen

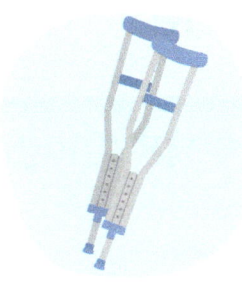 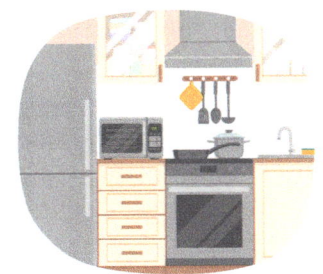 

8) ketchup

9) hockey

10) pocket

11) rocket

49

Listen to and write the phonograms.
Underline any multi-letter phonograms.

SCORE CORRECT RESCORE

6. WHAT DO ui, ue, AND ei SAY?

Learn:

- Write and say the sounds for multi-letter phonograms **ui**, **ue**, and **ei**.

- Read words with prefixes.

Vocabulary:

prefix [′prē fĭx] – a letter or group of letters added to the beginning of a base word

Listen and review.
Mark ☒ when done.

cr**ui**se   swims**ui**t

Write and say the sound.
Underline the multi-letter phonograms.

ui ui ui ui ui

ui

ue

purs**ue** cl**ue**s

Write and say the sound.
Underline the multi-letter phonograms.

ue

ue

weird   reindeer

Write and say the sounds.
Underline the multi-letter phonograms.

ei   ei   ei   ei   ei

ei   · ·   · ·   · ·   · ·

Read and write the words.

fruit

suit

swimsuit

1)

2)

3)

blue

due

glue

4)

5)

6)

Vowel team **ei** makes its first sound most of the time.

FIRST SOUND OF **ei**

 **Read and write the words.**

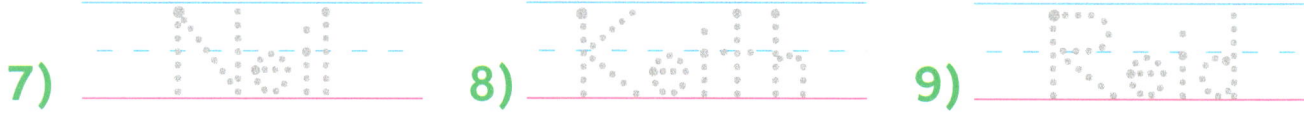

7) _____   8) _____   9) _____

SECOND SOUND OF **ei**

10) _____   11) _____   12) _____

WORKING WITH WORDS

A **prefix** is a letter or group of letters added to the beginning of a base word. Prefixes change the meaning of a word.

un – reverse or do the opposite of

zip

*un*zip

non – not

stop

*non*stop

Prefix Division: Separate base words from prefixes by dividing after the prefix.

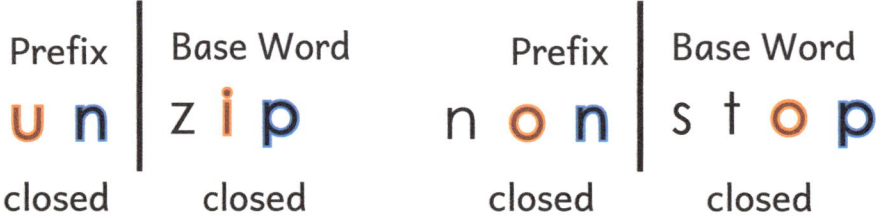

Prefix	Base Word		Prefix	Base Word
u n	z i p		n o n	s t o p
closed	closed		closed	closed

Prefixes like *un* and *non* are common. You will see them often. Practice dividing words after them.

*un*zip   *non*stop

Divide and read the words.
Then, circle the correct picture. Remember, underline the multi-letter phonograms first.

8) nonslip

9) unplug

10) unwrap

11) nonstick

WRITING PHONOGRAM REVIEW

 **Listen to and write the phonograms.**
Underline any multi-letter phonograms.

PHONOGRAM REVIEW

 **Listen to and circle the correct phonograms.**

1)  oi   ie   igh

2)  ea   t   ed

3)  nk   ng   n

4)  ey   oe   ay

5)  ey   oi   oy

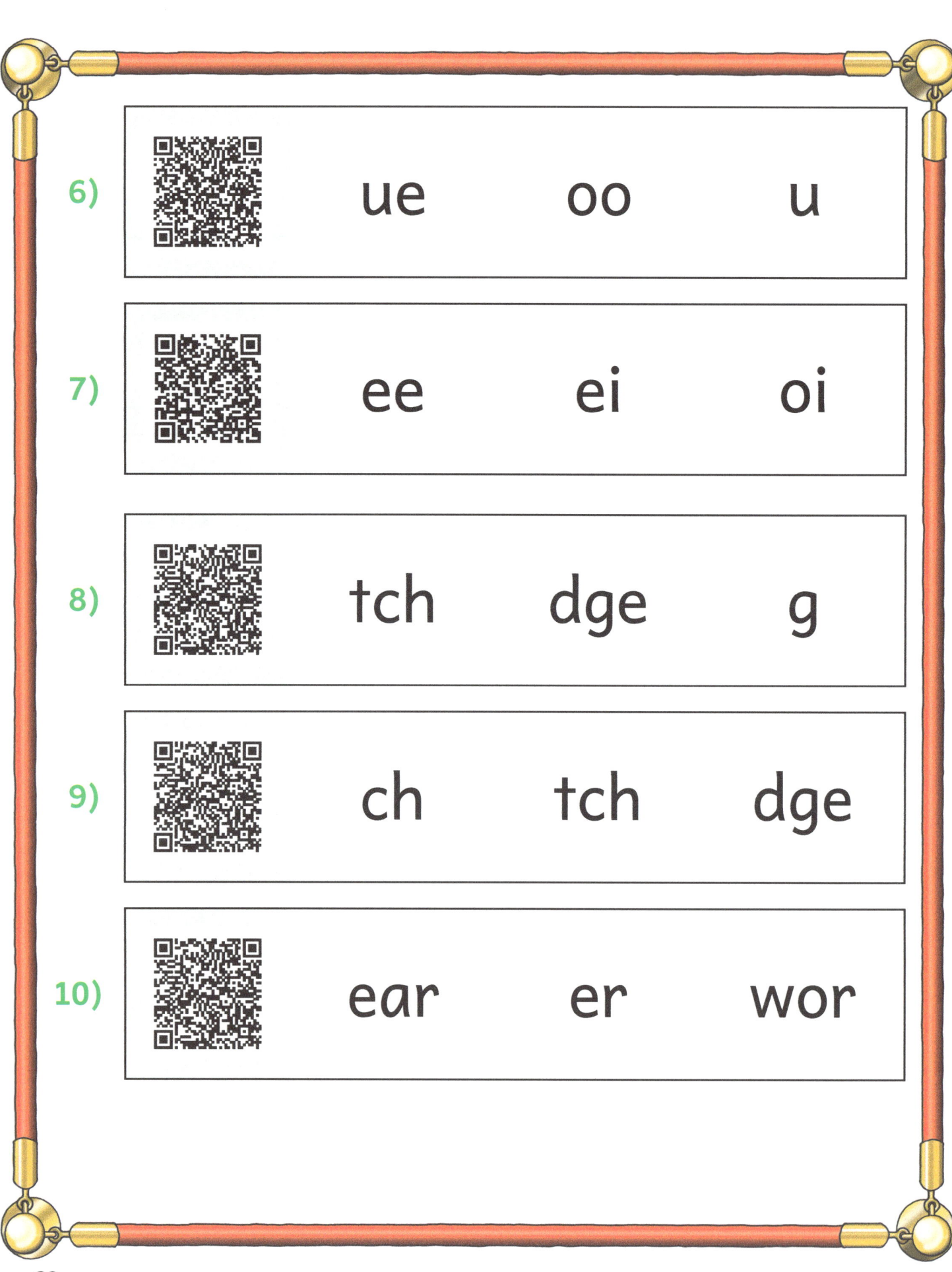

6) ue   oo   u

7) ee   ei   oi

8) tch   dge   g

9) ch   tch   dge

10) ear   er   wor

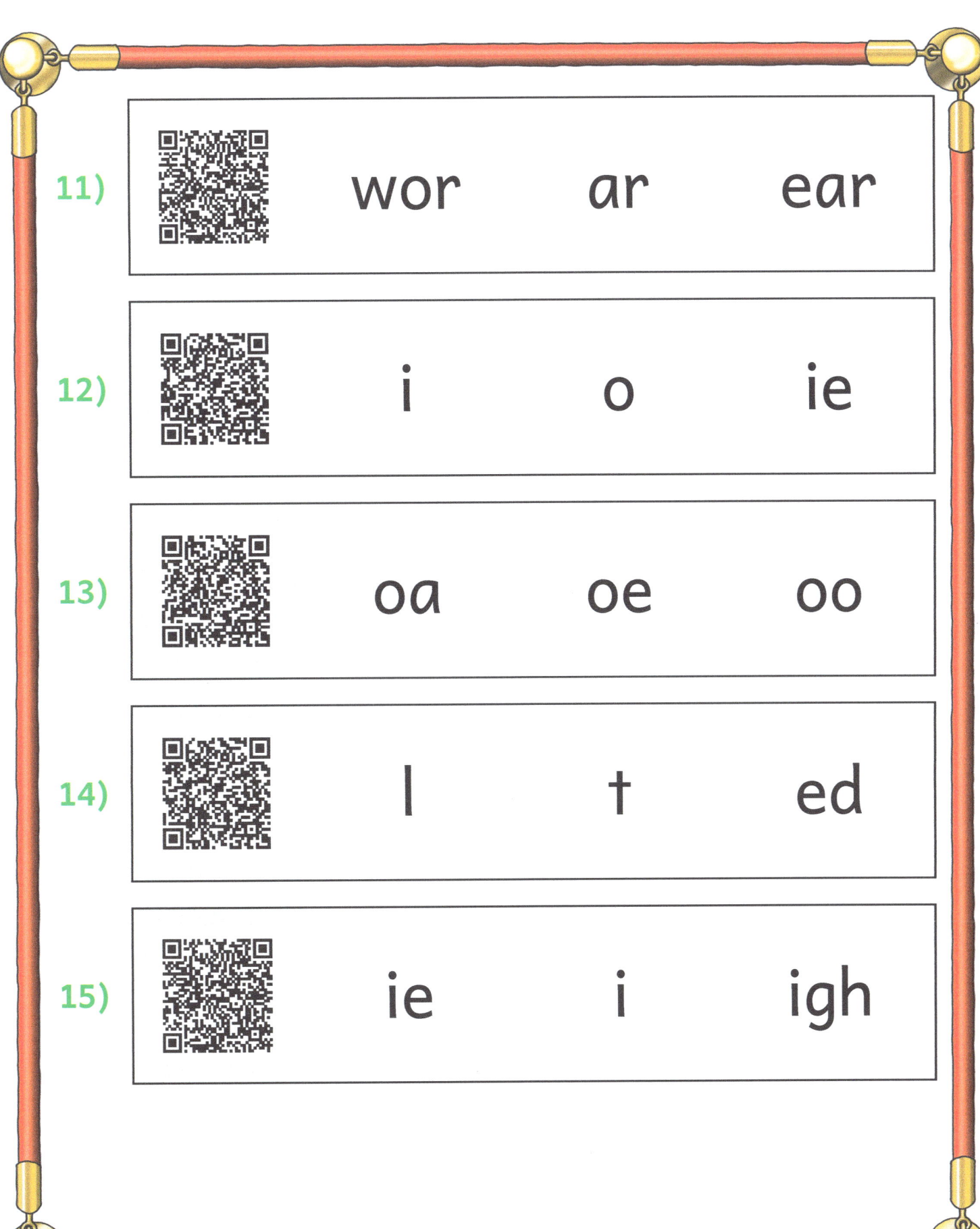

11) wor   ar   ear

12) i   o   ie

13) oa   oe   oo

14) l   t   ed

15) ie   i   igh

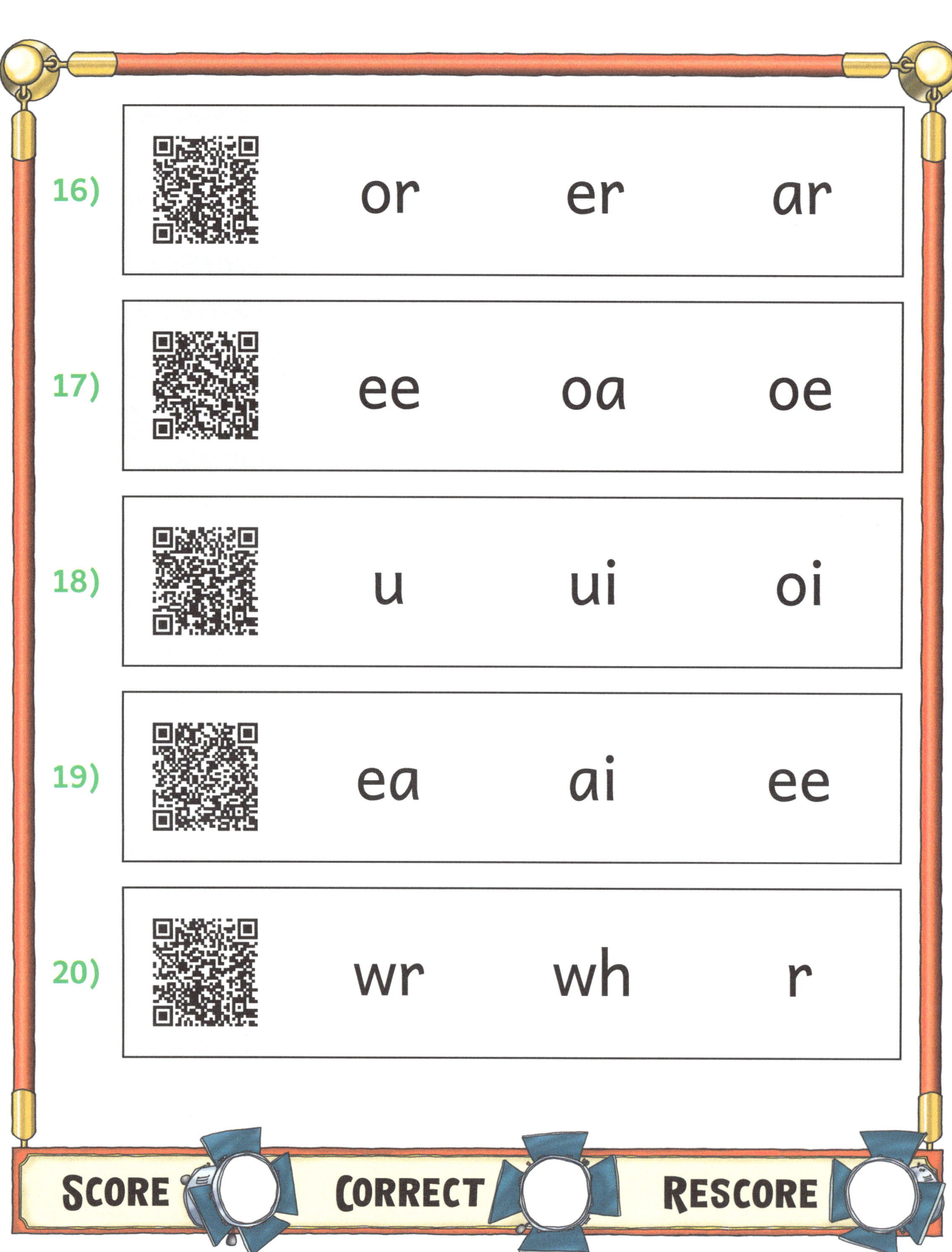

16) or   er   ar

17) ee   oa   oe

18) u   ui   oi

19) ea   ai   ee

20) wr   wh   r

SCORE   CORRECT   RESCORE

READER 6: "Fun on a Boat"

Before you read, practice these words.

 **Read and trace the words.**

1) water

2) writer

3) letter

4) fudge

5) edge

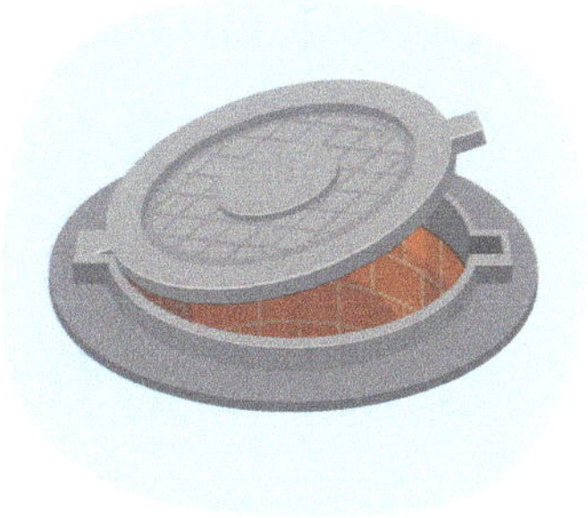

6) hatch

7) wagon

8) turkey

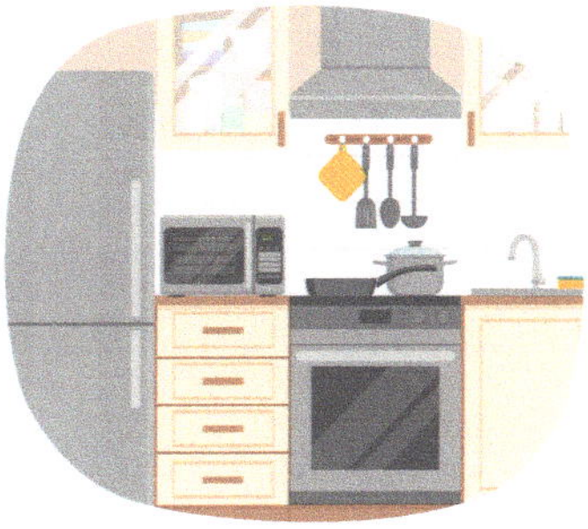

9) kitchen

Reader 6

Fun on a Boat

Choose the correct answers.

10) What did Zip do on the boat?
   - ○ write letters
   - ○ row the boat
   - ○ wave a flag

11) What did Pip see in the water?
   - ○ a dolphin
   - ○ a shark
   - ○ a whale

12) What did everyone do at the end?
   - ○ dance the Hokey Pokey
   - ○ go swimming
   - ○ take a nap

Phonogram Test 11

Listen to and write the correct phonograms.
Underline any multi-letter phonograms.

1)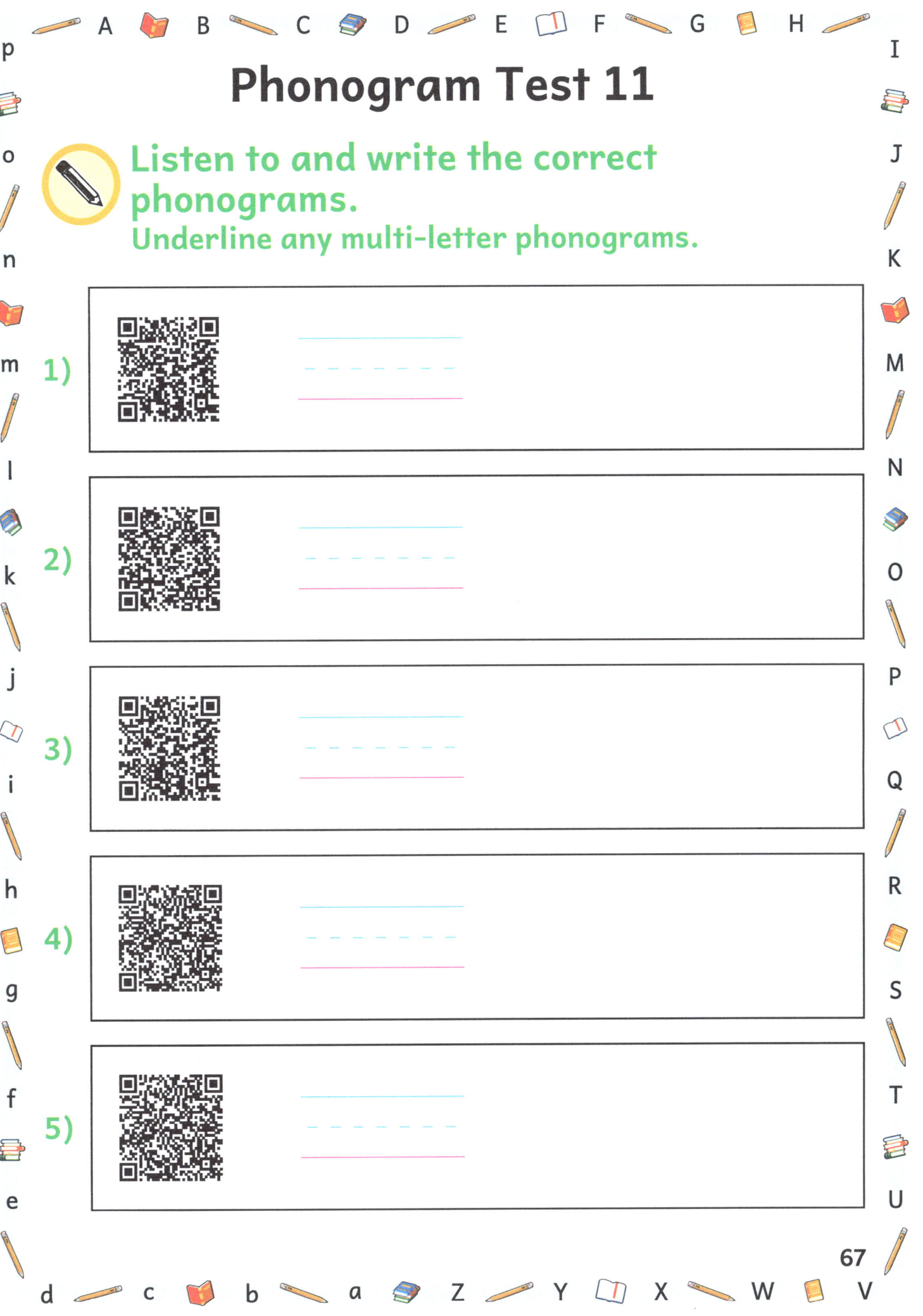

2)

3)

4)

5)

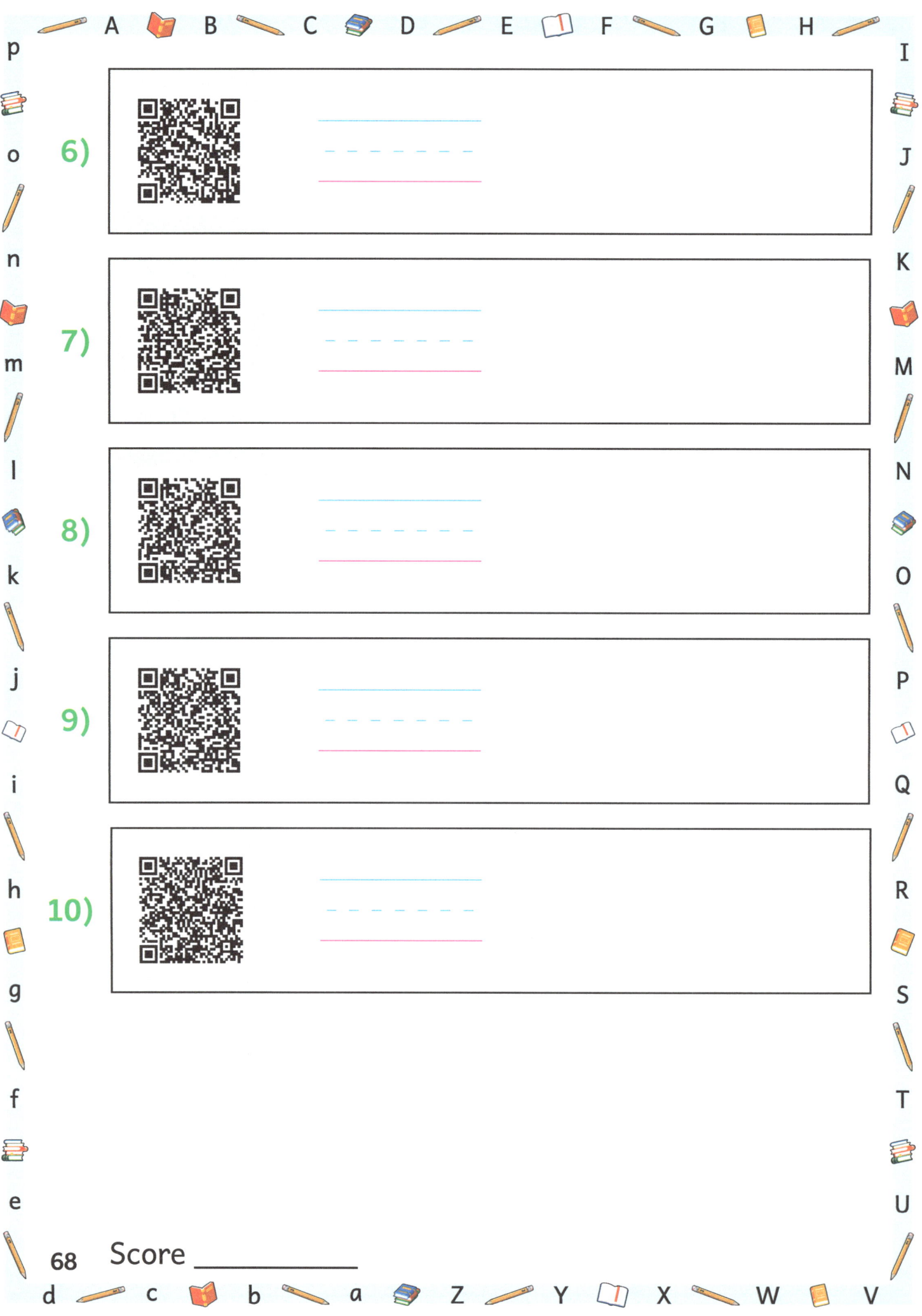

6)

7)

8)

9)

10)

Score _____

7. WHAT DO kn AND gn SAY?

Learn:

- Write and say the sounds for multi-letter phonograms **kn** and **gn**.

- Read words with prefixes.

Listen and review.
Mark ⊠ when done.

knock   **kn**ob

Write and say the sound.
Underline the multi-letter phonograms.

kn

kn

70

gnu   rei**gn**

Write and say the sound.
Underline the multi-letter phonograms.

gn gn gn gn gn

gn

Read and write the words.

knot	knife	kneel

1)

2)

3)

gnat	gnome	gnaw

4)

5)

6)

WORKING WITH WORDS

You will learn two more prefixes. They are open syllables.

re – again or back

heat   reheat

pre – before

school   preschool

Reading Rules

Prefix Division: Separate base words from prefixes by dividing after the prefix.

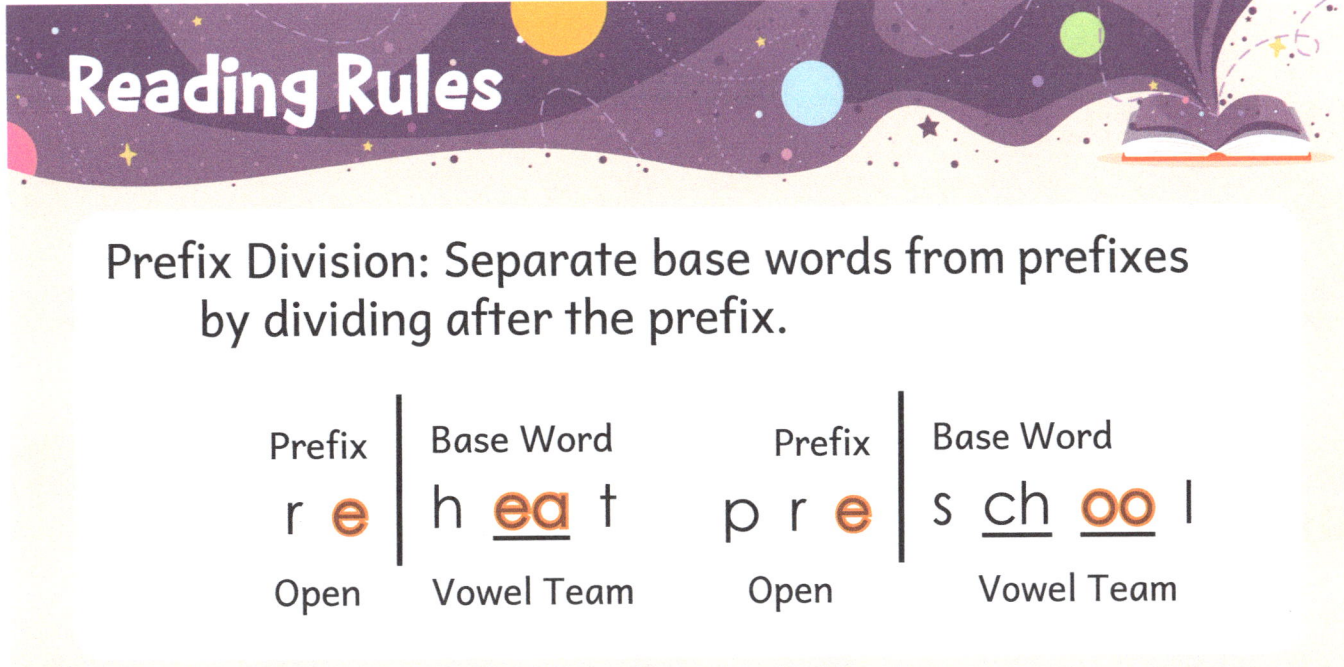

Divide and read the words.
Then, write the base words on the lines. Remember,
underline the multi-letter phonograms first.

7) refill

8) prepay

9) preshow

10) repaint

 **Listen to and write the phonograms.**
Underline any multi-letter phonograms.

SCORE   CORRECT   RESCORE

8. WHAT DO **ough** AND **eigh** SAY?

Learn:

- Write and say the sounds for multi-letter phonograms **ough** and **eigh**.

- Read words with prefixes.

**Listen and review.
Mark ☒ when done.**

ough

d**ough**nut thr**ough**
r**ough** c**ough**
th**ough**t dr**ough**t

 ## Write and say the sounds.
Underline the multi-letter phonograms.

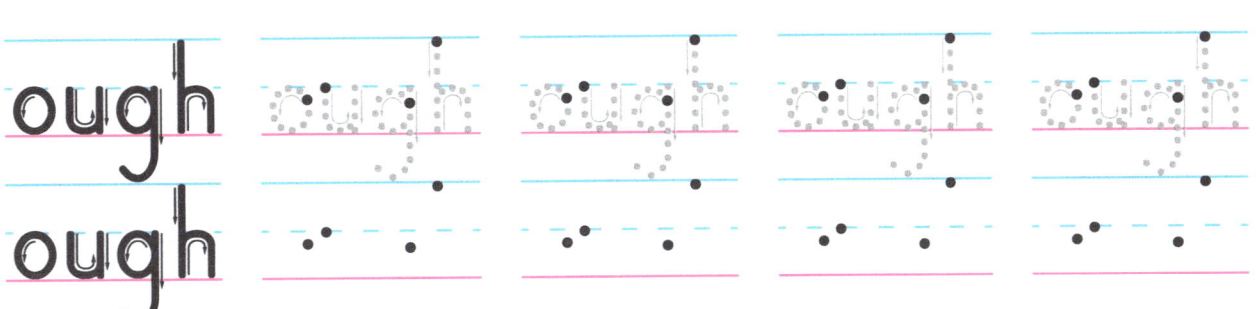

ough

ough

eigh

eight n**eigh**bors

Write and say the sounds.
Underline the multi-letter phonograms.

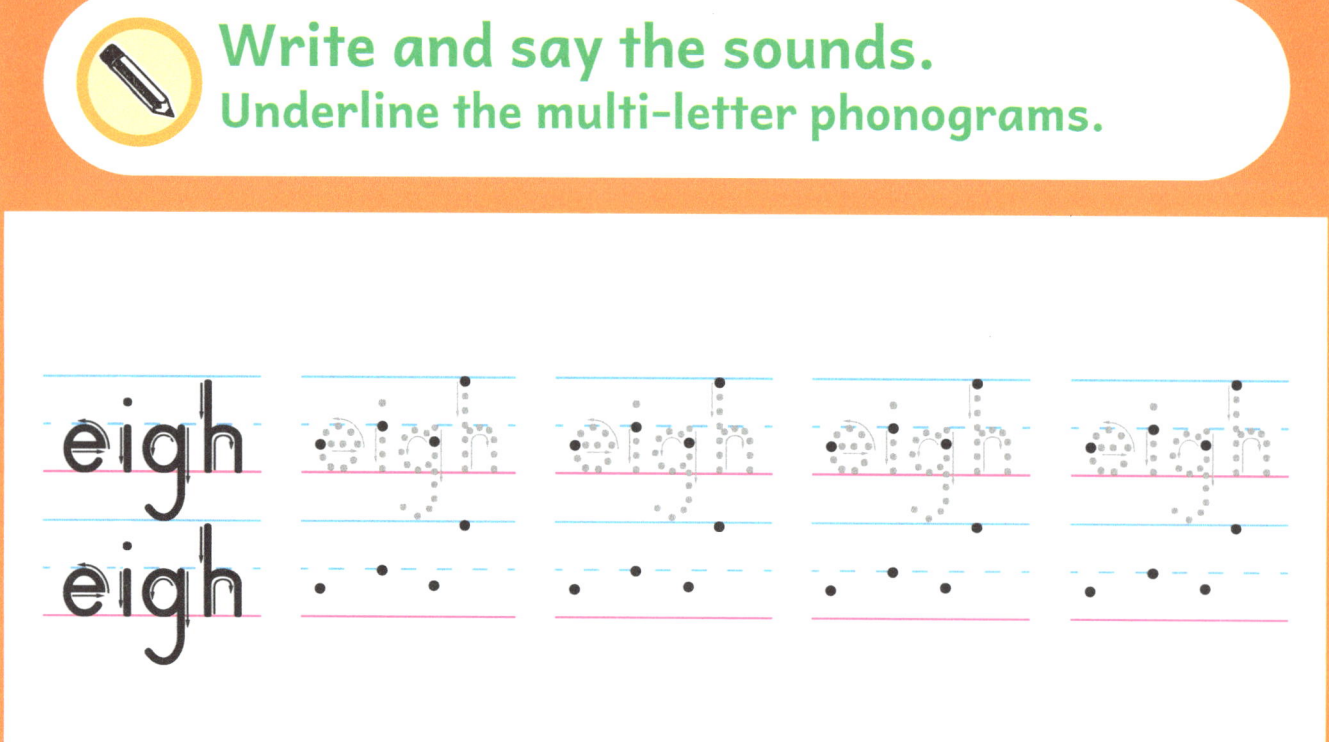

eigh

eigh

Vowel teams **ough** and **eigh** can be tricky.

The good news is that we only use them in a few words!

 **Trace the words.**
Then, use the rhyming words to read the sentences.

1)

Joe throws the

dough.

2)

Sue flew through the sky.

3)

Scruff will puff up to look

tough.

4)

Dot  a cot for Spot.

5)

The gray dogs pull the sleigh.

WORKING WITH WORDS

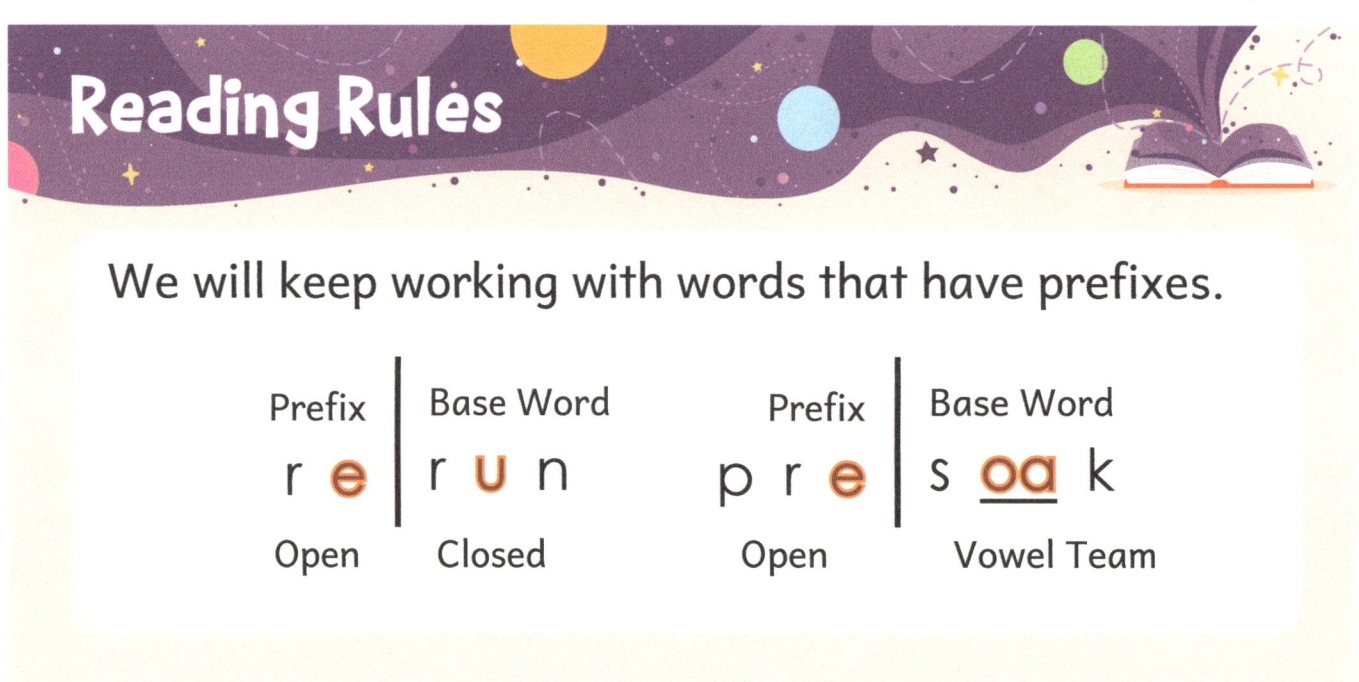

Reading Rules

We will keep working with words that have prefixes.

Prefix	Base Word		Prefix	Base Word
r e	r u n		p r e	s oa k
Open	Closed		Open	Vowel Team

Divide and read the words with prefixes.

Remember, underline the multi-letter phonograms first.

renew

pretest

remix

unwell

nonfan

unjust

prewash

undo

nonskid

resell

preset

nonmeat

 **Listen to and write the phonograms.**
Underline any multi-letter phonograms.

SCORE · CORRECT · RESCORE

ACTIVITY: Everyday Words

Read, trace, and write the words.

Read	Trace	Write
know	know	
they	they	
night	night	
right	right	
their	their	

9. WHAT DO **ti**, **ci**, AND **si** SAY?

Learn:

- Write and say the sounds for multi-letter phonograms **ti**, **ci**, and **si**.

- Read words with final stable syllables.

Vocabulary:

final stable syllables *[ˊfĭ nŭl ˊstā bŭl ˊsĭ lŭ bŭlz]* – syllables that are used in many words as the last syllable

Listen and review.
Mark ☒ when done.

ac**ti**on   mo**ti**on

Write and say the sound.
Underline the multi-letter phonograms.

ti   ti

ti   ti

spe**ci**al   magi**ci**an

Write and say the sound.
Underline the multi-letter phonograms.

ci   ci   ci   ci   ci

ci

si

exten**si**on   televi**si**on

Write and say the sounds.
Underline the multi-letter phonograms.

si   si   si   si   si

si   ..   ..

WORKING WITH WORDS

The phonograms **ti**, **si**, and **ci** are only used in final stable syllables. **Final stable syllables** are used in many words as the last syllable.

They are called final because they are at the end of a word. They are called stable because the sounds stay the same.

 **Listen to these words with common final stable syllables.**

cau**tion**

expan**sion**

gla**cial**

Reading Rules

Final Stable Syllable Division: Divide a word before a final stable syllable.

Vowel Team   FSS

Open   FSS

Divide and read words with the final stable syllables *tion*, *sion*, and *cial*.
Remember, underline the multi-letter phonograms first.

nation

tension

social

option

fiction

action

mansion

portion

facial

station

auction

pension

 **Listen to and write the phonograms.**
Underline any multi-letter phonograms.

SCORE   CORRECT   RESCORE

PHONOGRAM REVIEW

? Listen to and circle the correct phonograms.

1)  f   ph   th

2)  ew   ui   ue

3)  ch   th   tch

4)  ei   ey   ee

5)  eigh   ea   ey

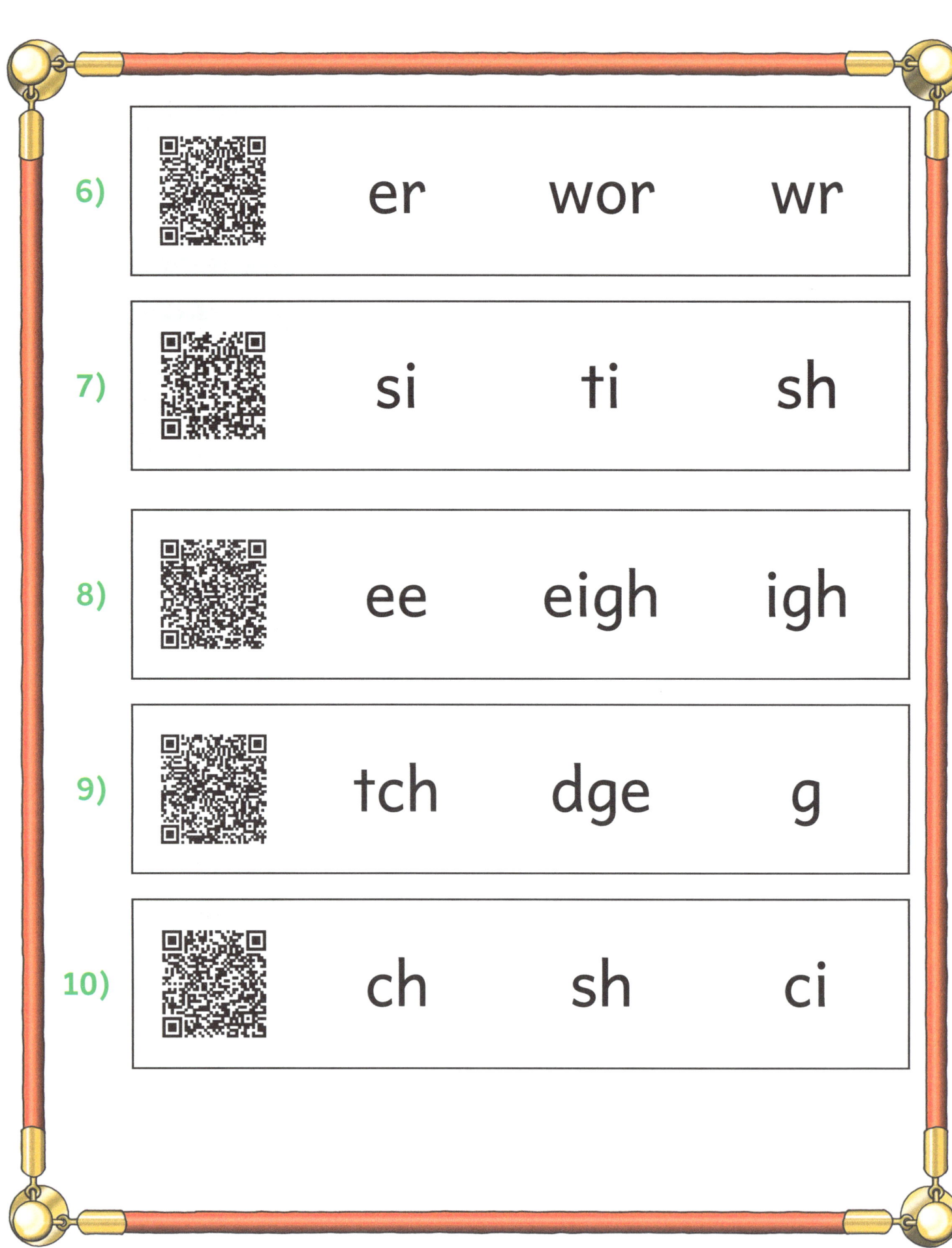

6) er   wor   wr

7) si   ti   sh

8) ee   eigh   igh

9) tch   dge   g

10) ch   sh   ci

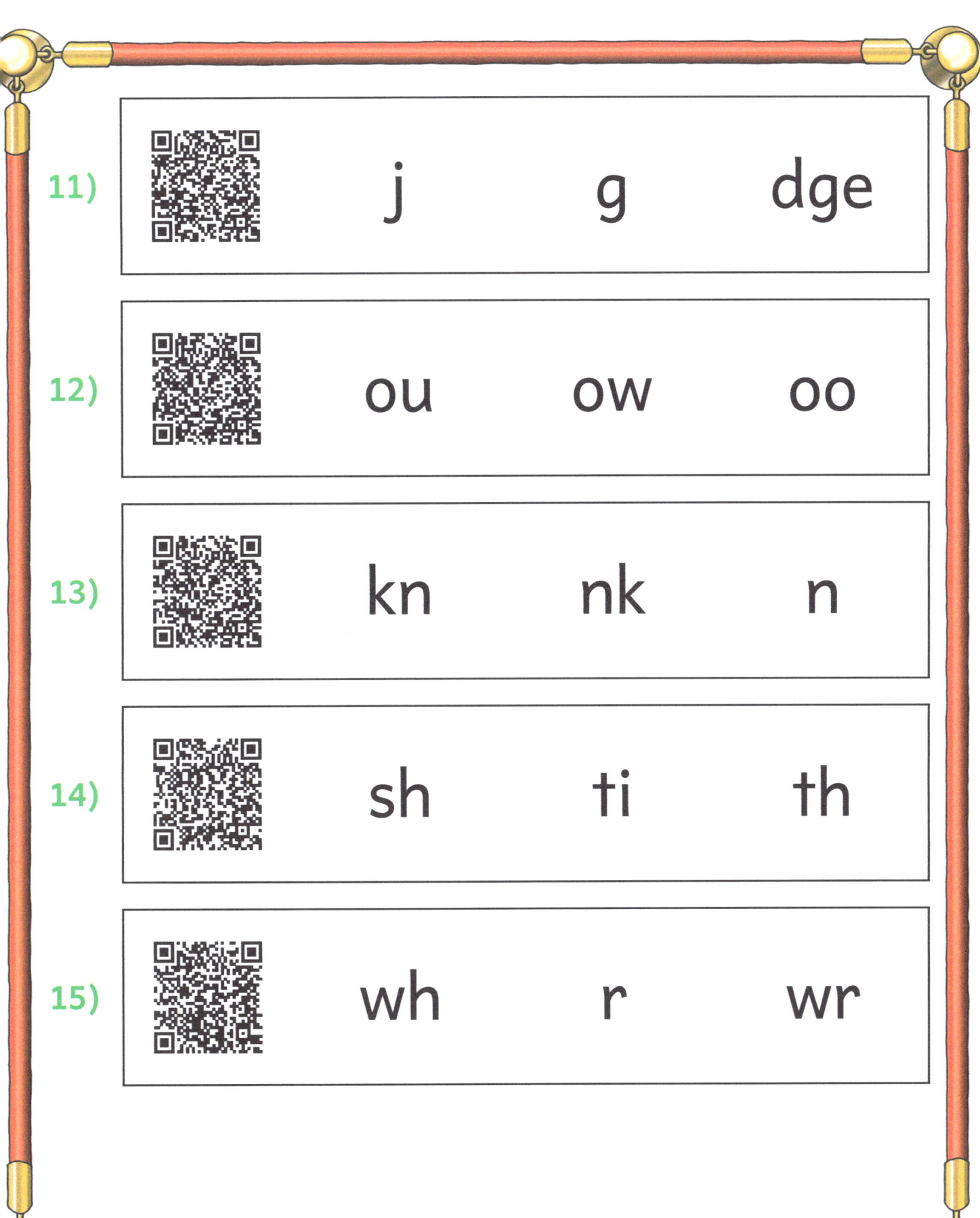

11) j   g   dge

12) ou   ow   oo

13) kn   nk   n

14) sh   ti   th

15) wh   r   wr

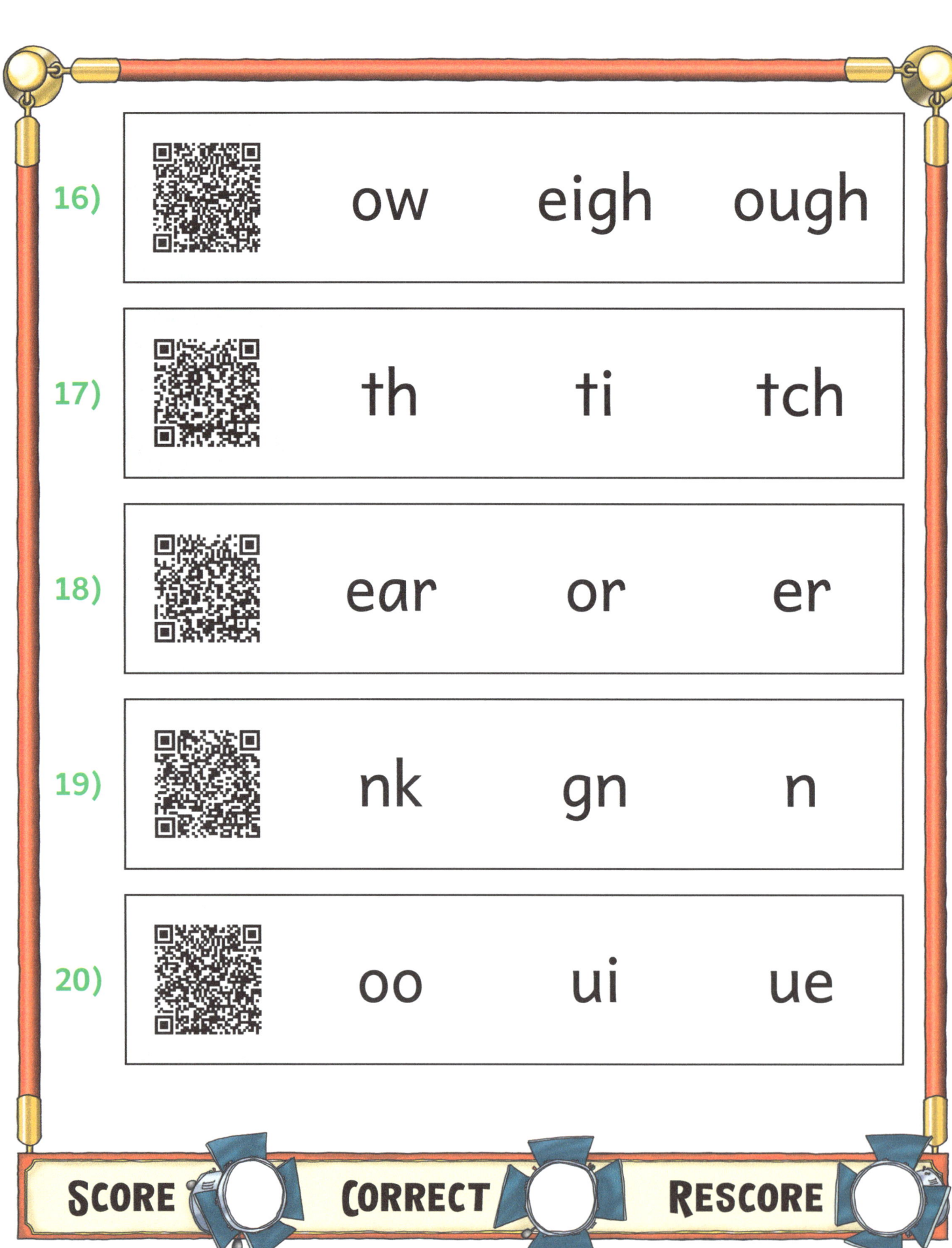

16) ow   eigh   ough

17) th   ti   tch

18) ear   or   er

19) nk   gn   n

20) oo   ui   ue

Before you read, practice these words.

 **Read and trace the words.**

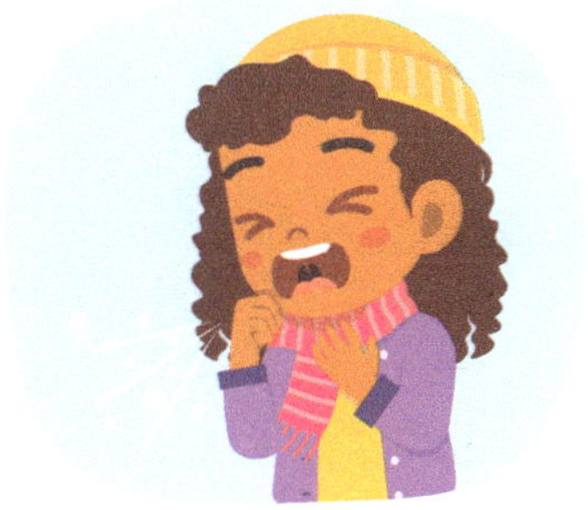

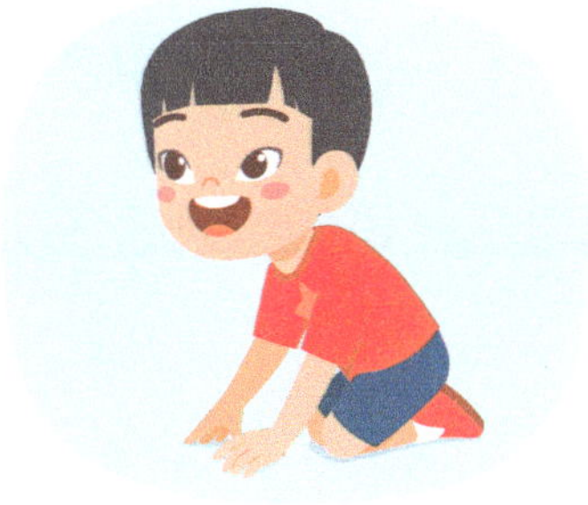

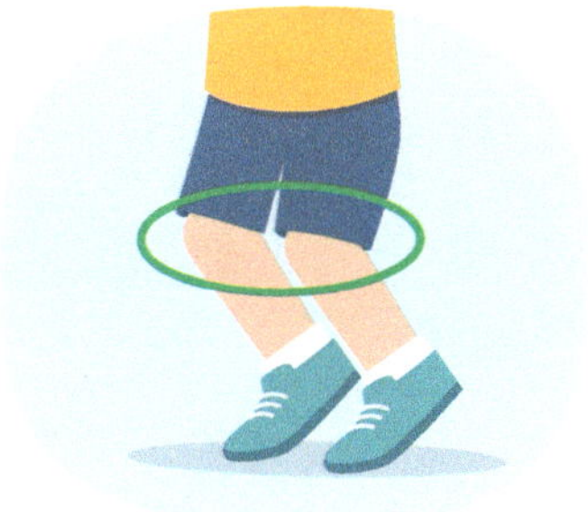

1) cough

2) kneel

3) knees

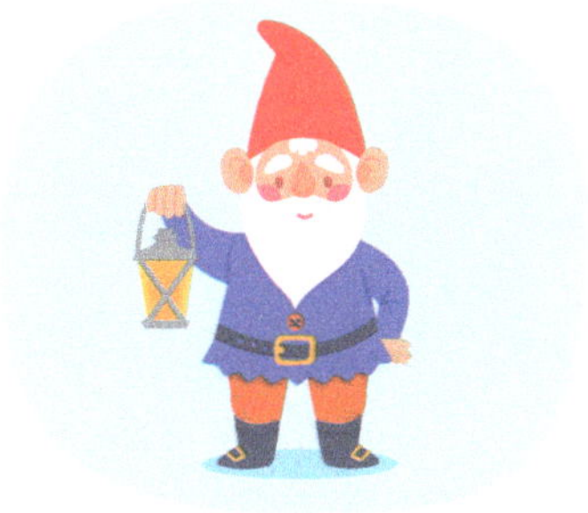

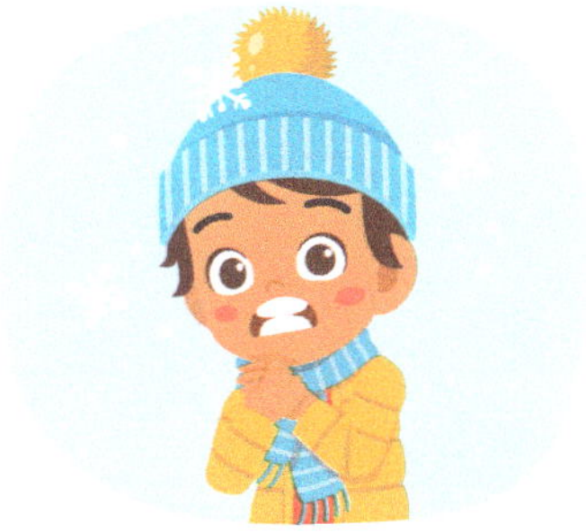

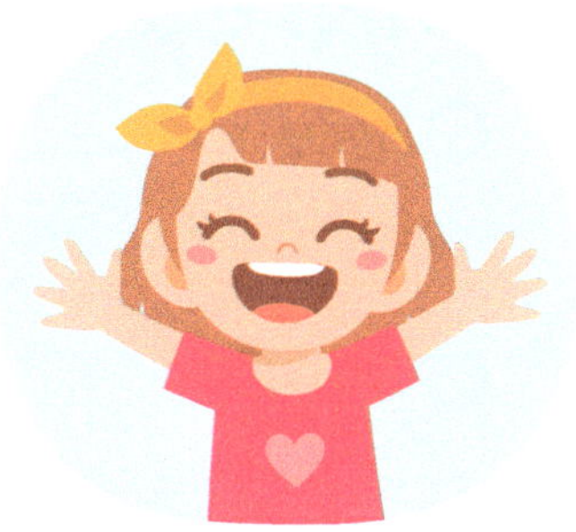

4) gnome

5) chilly

6) happy

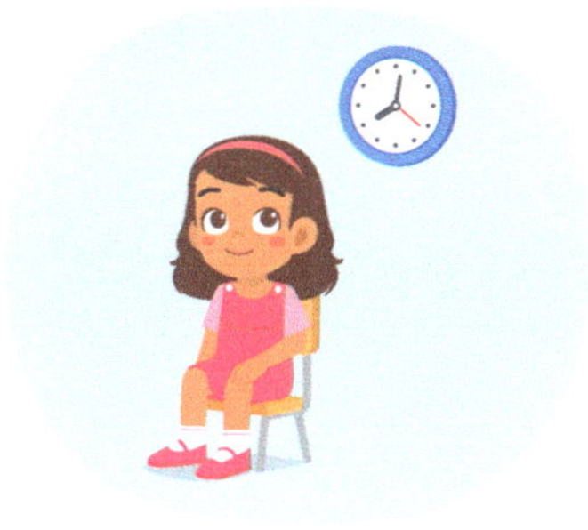

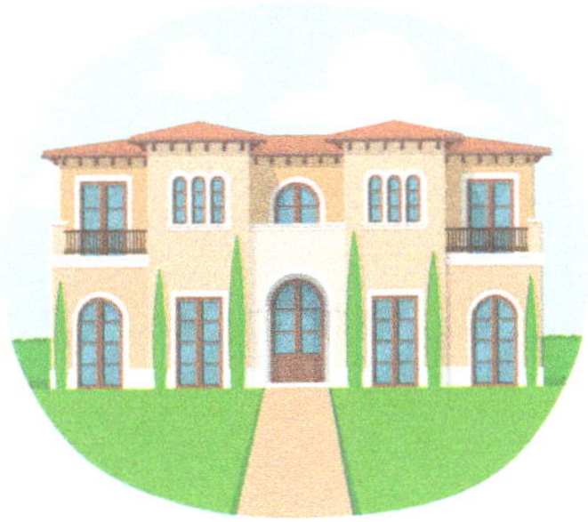

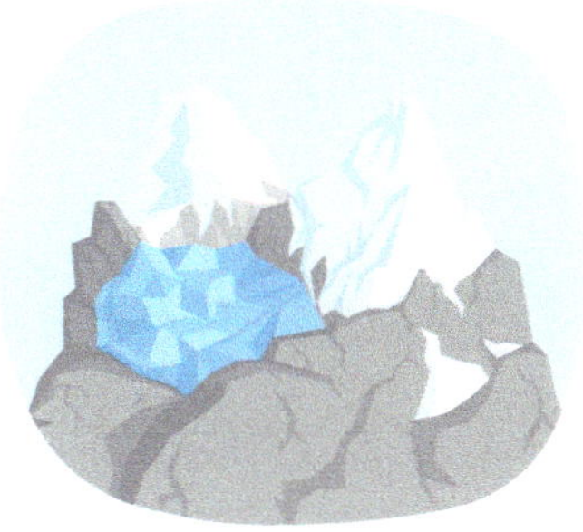

7) patient

8) mansion

9) glacier

Reader 7

We Surf the Waves

Choose the correct answers.

10) What did Ottie and Zip want to do?
- ○ swim
- ○ surf
- ○ float

11) Why did Pip not want to get in the water?
- ○ It was too cold.
- ○ There were too many fish.
- ○ He wanted to go home.

12) What is one thing the characters saw?
- ○ a monkey
- ○ a knight
- ○ a sleigh

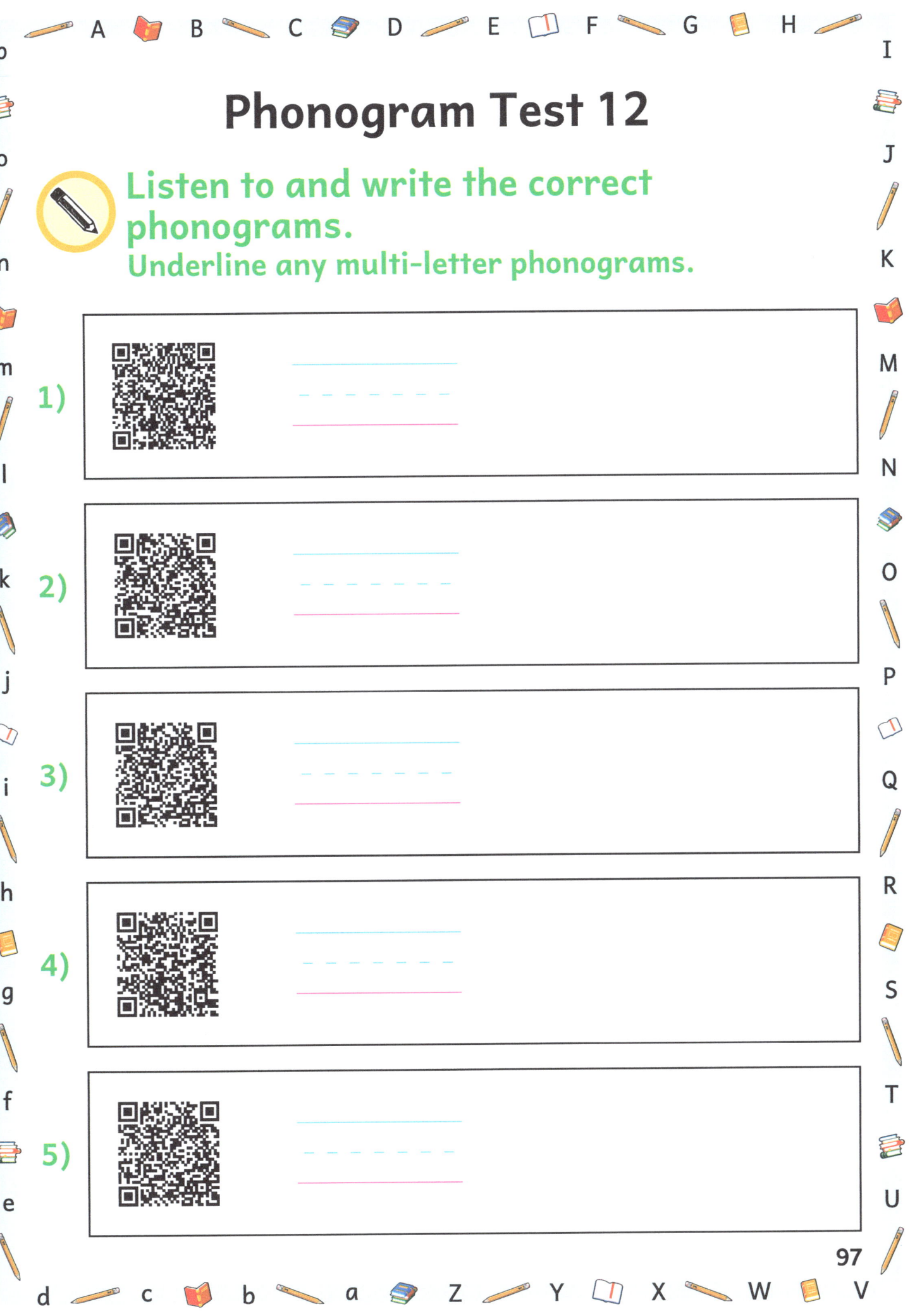

Phonogram Test 12

Listen to and write the correct phonograms.
Underline any multi-letter phonograms.

1)

2)

3)

4)

5)

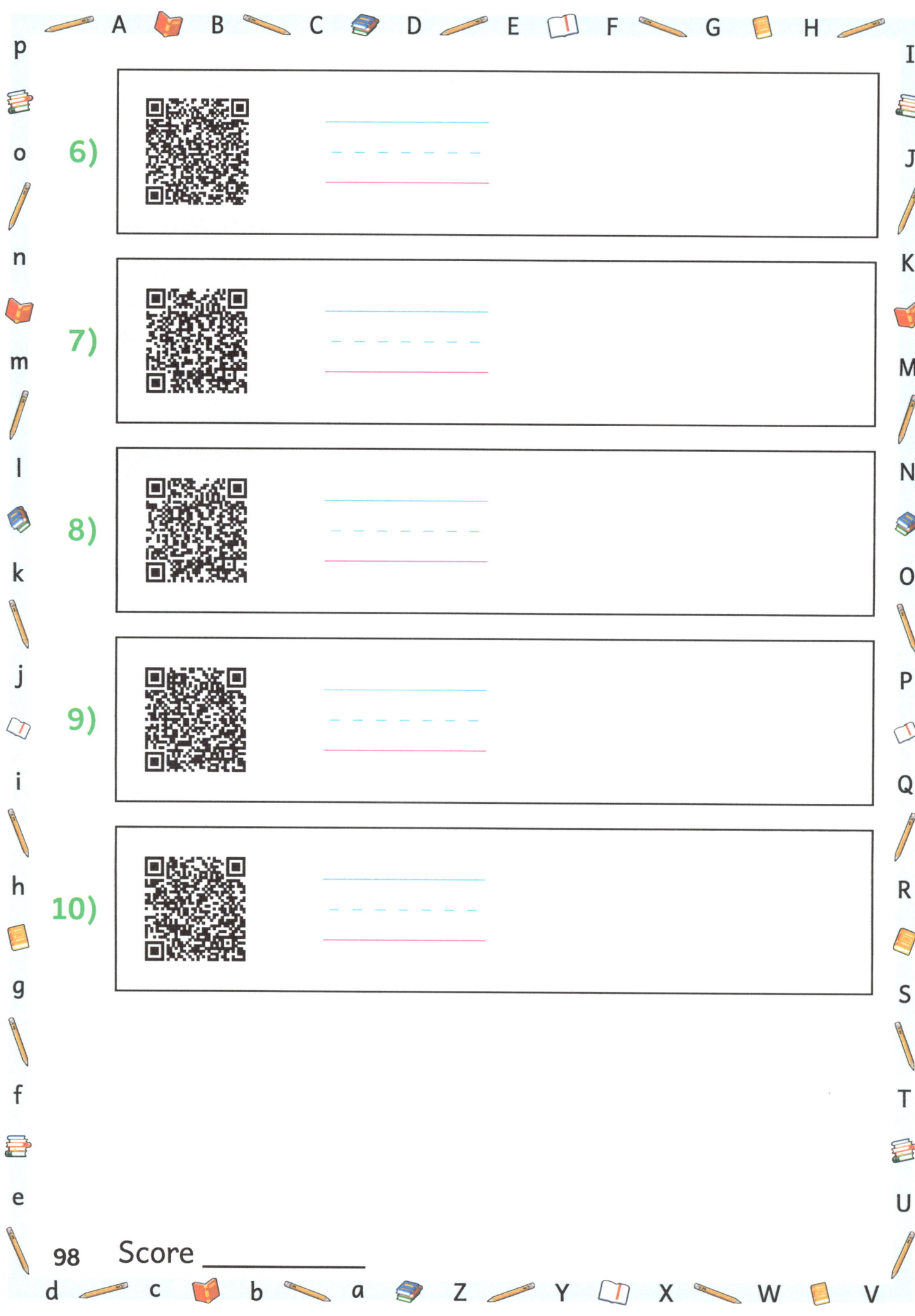

Score _____